Israel and the Legacy of Harry S. Truman

Israel and the Legacy of Harry S. Truman
The Truman Legacy Series, Volume 3

Based in part on the Third Truman Legacy Symposium
Harry Truman and the Quest for Peace in the Middle East
May 14, 2005
Key West, Florida

Edited by
Michael J. Devine
Robert P. Watson
Robert J. Wolz

ISRAEL and the
LEGACY of
HARRY S. TRUMAN

Edited by

Michael J. Devine
Robert P. Watson
Robert J. Wolz

Volume 3
Truman State University Press

Cover photo, section pages: Dr. Chaim Weizmann, president of Israel, presents a Torah to Truman during a visit to the White House on May 25, 1948 (TL 59-8).

Cover design: Jennifer Wiemer
Type: Garamond Light, ITC Garamond is a registered trademark of International Typeface Corporation; Bauer Text Initials, copyright Phil's Fonts.
Printed by: Thomson-Shore, Dexter, Michigan USA

Library of Congress Cataloging-in-Publication Data
Truman Legacy Symposium (3rd : 2004 : Key West, Fla.)
Israel and the legacy of Harry S. Truman / edited by Michael J. Devine, Robert P. Watson, Robert J. Wolz.
    p. cm. — (Truman legacy series ; v. 3)
"Based in part on the Third Truman Legacy Symposium : Harry Truman and civil rights, 14-15 May 2004, Key West, Florida."
Includes bibliographical references and index.
ISBN 978-1-931112-80-2 (pbk. : alk. paper)
1. Truman, Harry S., 1884–1972—Influence—Congresses. 2. United States—Foreign relations—Israel—Congresses. 3. Israel—Foreign relations—United States—Congresses. 4. United States—Foreign relations—1945–1953—Congresses. 5. Israel—History—1948–1967—Congresses. I. Devine, Michael J., 1945- II. Watson, Robert P., 1962- III. Wolz, Robert J. IV. Title.
    E814.T85 2004
    973.918—dc22

                                                                        2008025518

"But don't think the decision to recognize Israel was an easy one."
—Harry S. Truman, 1964
Screen Gems Collection, MP2002–344

Contents

HARRY S. TRUMAN, JEWS, AND THE RECOGNITION OF ISRAEL

REFLECTIONS ON THE MIDDLE EAST SINCE 1948

ILLUSTRATIONS

Preface

The region of the Middle East known as the Holy Land has vexed the leaders of nations for centuries. At the close of World War II, the new United States president, Harry S. Truman, found himself facing volatile and complex international situations left in the war's aftermath. The rising tensions with the Soviet Union, the new challenges posed by the development of nuclear weapons, the colossal civil war in China, the threatened collapse of Western European economies, and the tide of national liberation sweeping across Africa and Southeast Asia all confronted President Truman during a period that he would later characterize in the title of the second volume of his memoirs, *Years of Trial and Hope.*

Among the crises Truman confronted in the postwar years was the question of Palestine, which was controlled by Britain under a United Nations mandate due to expire in 1948. For many generations Palestine had been primarily an Arab land, but Jews, motivated by religious fervor and a desire for a homeland, had settled there in ever-increasing numbers during the first half of the twentieth century. After the Holocaust, many thousands of the survivors wanted to immigrate to Palestine as well. As tensions between the Arabs and Jews rose, Palestine was on the verge of civil war by early 1948.

Escalating violence between Jews and Palestinian Arabs, the decision of the British to abandon Palestine when their United Nations mandate expired, increasing Soviet interest in the Middle East, and the ever-present American concern for ready access to vast Middle Eastern oil fields located in neighboring Arab countries all contributed to placing the question of a Jewish state at the forefront of Truman's foreign policy agenda. Moreover, as 1948 was an election year, domestic politics had to be taken into consideration. Significant numbers of Jewish voters in key states, particularly New York, Pennsylvania, and Illinois, could be decisive in a close presidential election where every electoral vote would be precious, and Jewish American voters appeared nearly unanimous in their support of a Jewish homeland in Palestine. While several leading Republicans, among them potential presidential candidates, had expressed public support for a Jewish state in Palestine, Truman's advisors were divided on the issue. The president's key foreign policy and defense policy advisors, including Secretary of State George C. Marshall and Defense Secretary James Forrestal, adamantly opposed the recognition of a Jewish state and the likely disruption of relations with Arab nations. The president faced a critical decision that he knew would exacerbate criticism of his administration and anger many of his closest advisors.

Truman recognized the State of Israel on May 14, 1948, at almost the instant its existence was announced, because he believed that his decision was fair. Reflecting on his decision a decade and a half later, Truman recalled, "What I was trying to do was find a homeland for the Jews and still be just with the Arabs."[1] He also believed that the existence of Israel would lead to eventual peace and prosperity in the Middle East.

Despite pleas from many in the pro-Israeli lobby, Truman provided only de facto recognition, insisting that elections must be held in Israel before de jure recognition could be provided, and he refused to lift the United States arms embargo affecting Israel. Furthermore, he would not recognize the ambitious borders the new state had claimed. "There was a lot of Jewish people against me because they wanted the whole of Palestine," Truman stated.[2] At the same time that Truman recognized the new State of Israel, he made it clear that he was fully prepared to recognize a Palestinian state, and he expected to do so as soon as an identifiable government came forward. However, the warfare that erupted on May 15 between Israel and its neighbors, Egypt, Syria, Jordan, Lebanon, and Iraq, and the resulting flow of Palestinian refugees prevented the establishment of a Palestinian state during Truman's presidency.

Truman was fully aware that the immigration of Jews to Palestine and the recognition of Israel would upset the Arab world, and he took steps to mitigate the damage. In July of 1946, he wrote to King Abdul Aziz Ibn Saud of Saudi Arabia, stating, "I am sincere in my belief that the admission to Palestine of 100,000 Jewish refugees this year would neither prejudice the rights and privileges of the Arabs now in Palestine nor constitute a change in the basic situation." Again, six months later, Truman sought to reassure the Saudi leader by stating that "in supporting the establishment of a Jewish National Home in Palestine" the objective of the United States was to preserve "the fundamental rights of both the Arab and Jewish population of Palestine," and to create conditions in which "Palestine Arabs and Jews alike shall prosper and shall lead lives free of any

kind of political or economic oppression."[3] Following the establishment of the State of Israel and the immediate outbreak of war, Truman sought to reconcile Arabs and Jews by urging Israeli leaders to
repatriate Palestinians displaced during the months of savage fighting.
Truman's pleas went nowhere. Israel did not respond to Truman's
argument that allowing just a fraction of the Arab refugees to return
to their homes would allow him "to continue his strong and warm
support for Israel and the efforts being made by its government to
establish its new political and economic structure on a firm basis."[4]

In October of 1948, Truman ordered American armed forces to
provide food, clothing, and medicine to Palestinian refugees. He also
offered United States support for one half of the costs of a United
Nations allocation of $32 million for Palestinian refugees. However,
the Truman administration demonstrated little support for the work
of the United Nations Trusteeship Council as it labored unsuccessfully over the final disposition of Jerusalem, and the ancient city
remained divided. When de jure recognition was finally extended to
the State of Israel on January 31, 1949, Truman, in a significant and
symbolic gesture, announced the recognition of Transjordan on the
same date. However, by this time the Truman administration was
preoccupied with rising Cold War tensions in Western Europe and
Asia, and it would be left to future U.S. presidents to continue the
pursuit of an elusive peace in the Middle East.

Most of the presentations published in this volume were first
delivered at a symposium entitled "Harry S. Truman and the Recognition of Israel," which took place in Key West, Florida, in May
2005. The third in a series of Truman Legacy symposia, the 2005 program sought to examine Truman's decision to recognize Israel in the
politically charged atmosphere of 1948. Scholars, former government
officials, and diplomats were invited to look at Truman's actions
from various perspectives and analyze how the president's personal
beliefs and policies, and his relationships with members of the Jewish
American community influenced his decisions.

The Truman Legacy Symposium in May 2005 was produced
through a partnership of the Harry S. Truman Library Institute for
National and International Affairs, the White House Studies Program of Florida Atlantic University, and the Truman Little White
House. Dr. Robert Watson, now with Lynn University, and many
staff at the Truman Little White House labored long hours to assure
the success of the symposium, and it was a delight to work with
them on this endeavor. The Tennessee Williams Theatre at Florida
Keys Community College proved to be a superb location for the

symposium. Support for the symposium was provided by Historic Tours of America, Monroe County Tourist Development Council, and the Lifelong Learning and Holocaust and Judaic Studies programs at Florida Atlantic University. The John D. Evans Foundation, Betty Zinman Foundation, and Larkin Family Charitable Trust all assisted in funding the program.

Special expressions of gratitude go to Ed Swift, Chris Belland, Piper Smith, and Monica Munoz of Historic Tours of America. Michael McPherson, Rebecca Tomlinson, and Lydia Estenoz of Florida Keys Community College assisted in logistics, as did Richard Yon of University of Florida, Scott Roley of the Truman Presidential Library, and Kathy Knotts of the Truman Library Institute. A special thank-you is also extended to Clifton Truman Daniel for his participation in the symposium.

We are especially appreciative of the labor provided by Bonnie Neeleman of the Truman Presidential Library, who typed and retyped numerous drafts and revisions of the manuscript for this book. Two additional Truman Presidential Library staffers provided valuable expertise. Dr. Ray Geselbracht offered excellent advice and editing assistance, as well as preparing the chronology presented in this volume. Dr. Randy Sowell, who was responsible for the bibliography, also edited the final draft of the manuscript.

> Michael J. Devine, Truman Presidential
> Library, Independence, Missouri
> Robert P. Watson, Lynn University,
> Boca Raton, Florida
> Robert J. Wolz, Harry S. Truman Little
> White House, Key West, Florida
> January 2008

Notes

[1] Screen Gems Collection, MP2002-344, Audio Visual Collection, Truman Library.

[2] Screen Gems Collection, MP2002-344, Audio Visual Collection, Truman Library.

[3] President Truman to the King of Saudi Arabia, July 13, 1946. *Foreign Relations of the United States.* Vol. 7, *The Near East and Africa, 1946* (Washington, DC; U.S. Government Printing Office, 1969), 646; and President Truman to the King of Saudi Arabia, January 24, 1947, *Foreign Relations: Near East and Africa, 1947,* 5: 1012-13.

[4] Fred H. Lawson, "Palestine," in *Harry S. Truman Encyclopedia.*

THE $64 QUESTION

John B. Judis

When he assumed the presidency in April 1945, Harry Truman inherited a war that was still raging in the Pacific, the stirrings of conflict with the Soviet Union over Eastern Europe, and an electorate weary of wartime austerity. But what sometimes befuddled him most was what was happening in British-controlled Palestine. During a meeting later that year with Truman's chiefs of mission in the Near East, Minister to Lebanon and Syria George Wadsworth, speaking on behalf of his colleagues, asked the president "what the American policy [was] toward political Zionism." "That is the $64 dollar question," Truman replied. According to the minutes of the meeting, Truman lamented that "this question was causing him and [Secretary of States James] Byrnes more trouble than almost any other question which is facing the United States."[1]

History has shown that Truman and Byrnes had good reason to be troubled. Of all the great questions that America faced after World War II, that of how to resolve the conflict between the Jews and Arabs of Palestine—and later the Israelis and the Palestinians—has proven to be the most unanswerable. Sixty years later, the conflict continues to rage, and the United States is no closer to answering Truman's $64 question of what the United States should do about it.

Why has this conflict proven to be so intractable? Current commentators locate the source of the difficulty in what has happened since the Truman years. Some blame the Arabs and the Palestinians for their "extremist and shortsighted leadership which consistently rejected all compromise solutions." Others, pointing to the Israeli occupation of Palestinian lands, charge that the Israelis are "victims" who became "victimizers." And still others blame the continuing stalemate on a feckless diplomacy by the principal outside actor in the region, the United States.[2]

Although these different explanations are the subject of a sometimes fierce debate, there is truth in each one of them. The Palestinians have repeatedly rejected offers for compromise—only to accept them later after they were no longer being offered. That happened, notably, in 1947, 1979, and 2000. The Israelis, for their part, have been oblivious, if not hostile, to Palestinian nationalism and after the Six-Day War took control of, and began building settlements on, what remained of Arab Palestine. And American administrations have periodically either downplayed Arab threats to Israel—for instance, on the eve of the Six-Day War—or ignored or even encouraged Israeli attempts to create a "greater Israel."

But part of the reason that the conflict is intractable is what happened before and during the Truman years. By the time Truman decided to recognize Israel in May 1948, much of the groundwork for the subsequent rocket attacks, intifadas, assassinations, bulldozed villages, all-out wars, and illegal settlements had already been laid. The failure of Palestinian leadership was already evident during the revolt against the British in the 1930s, and Israel's territorial ambitions, which seemed to surface suddenly after the Six-Day War in 1967, go back to Zionist visions of the early 1900s. As for American policy, the equivocation and indecision and the reluctance to use American power to achieve peace between the two parties became fully evident during the Truman years.

What follows is necessarily a cursory survey of a century of conflict, but it is intended as a historical backdrop to the essays in this collection, which detail the special role that the Truman administration played in Israel's founding. Understanding what went before Truman's years in office puts into relief the obstacles that he faced in answering his $64 question. And looking at what happened afterwards shows the extent to which the difficulties he encountered have persisted into the present century.

A HISTORIC DEBATE

In 1896, Austrian playwright and journalist Theodor Herzl published *The Jewish State*. Like many middle-class European Jews, Herzl, who grew up in Budapest and Vienna, had believed that Jews would eventually either be assimilated into European society or convert to Christianity, but the pogroms in Russia of the early 1880s, his own encounter with anti-Semitism at the University of Vienna, and finally the Dreyfus Affair in France convinced him that European Jews were destined to remain a persecuted minority. Herzl realized that while Jews might see themselves as voluntary members of a religious group, they were in fact treated by Europeans as an alien people or nation. Herzl concluded that they could only escape persecution by acknowledging their existence as a national group and founding a state of their own in which they were the dominant majority. Herzl suggested either Palestine or Argentina; he organized the First Zionist Congress in Basel in 1897 and members of the new movement decided on Palestine.

There were two factions in this movement: the one, political Zionism, led by Herzl and later Chaim Weizmann, sought to secure a Jewish state diplomatically through the sponsorship of an imperial power; the other, cultural Zionism, led by the Eastern European Lovers of Zion, sought to encourage immigration to Palestine and advocated the creation of a new Hebrew-speaking Jewish culture. On the eve of World War I, about 60,000 Jews lived amidst about 750,000 Arabs in Palestine. About half of those Jews were recent immigrants inspired by cultural Zionism. But in 1917, the two factions were united when Weizmann, promoting a Jewish state as an "Asiatic Belgium" that would be a buffer between imperial Britain and the Arab Middle East, secured the support of the British cabinet for the establishment after the war of a "national home for the Jewish people in Palestine."[3]

The cabinet's declaration, issued in the form of a letter from British Foreign Secretary Arthur Balfour to Lord Rothschild, contained two important ambiguities and one significant omission that would become the basis of conflict among Jews, Arabs, and the British. First, the Balfour Declaration deliberately referred to a "national home" rather than a "state," out of deference to Britain's Arab allies in the region; and secondly, while Zionists themselves already envisioned a Jewish state of Palestine, the declaration talked of a home in Palestine.[4] At the same time, the declaration omitted any specific reference to the national rights of the Arabs already living in Palestine. Instead, it merely pledged to respect the "civil and religious rights of existing non-Jewish communities in Palestine."[5]

In other words, the British commitment to a Jewish Palestine was not unequivocal—and British equivocation after 1939 would lead to a clash between the Jews and the British. By the same token, the British simply did not recognize Palestine's Arabs as a people worthy of self-determination. That was reflected in Balfour's view that "Zionism, be it right or wrong, good or bad, is rooted in age-long traditions, in present needs, in future hopes, [and is] of far greater import than the desires and prejudices of the 700,000 Arabs who now inhabit that ancient land."[6] That attitude would lead later to clashes between the Arabs and the British and between the Arabs and the Jews.

The thrust of the Balfour Declaration was later included in the 1921 League of Nations mandate, which created Palestine alongside Transjordan and put Britain in charge of it. Jews were represented in Palestine by a protogovernmental body, the Jewish Agency. With British encouragement and through the efforts of the Jewish Agency, Jewish immigration began to pick up during the 1920s and to accelerate in the 1930s, as Hitler gained power in Germany. By 1941, there would be almost 500,000 Jews in Palestine, making up 30 percent of the population.

By contrast, the Arabs of Palestine possessed under the mandate no formal representation nor status as a colonized people. That stirred deep resentments among the Arabs. The lack of any organized political representation—such as the Iraqis or Jordanians or Egyptians enjoyed under British rule—deprived Palestine's Arabs of the institutions on the basis of which they could have constructed a national leadership. As historian Rashid Khalidi has argued, many of the failures in Palestinian leadership—from the grand mufti of the 1930s to Yasir Arafat of the 1990s—go back to the experience of Palestine's Arabs under British rule.[7]

ROOTS OF UNREST

In the nineteenth century, what had historically been Palestine was part of the Ottoman Empire. The first stirrings of Palestinian nationalism occurred in response to the Young Turk rebellion of 1908, but they were largely directed at creating a greater Syria that would include Palestine. After the British carved out Palestine, and Jewish immigration began in earnest—buoyed by the Balfour Declaration and the League mandate—the Arabs of Palestine began to identify themselves as "Palestinians" and to advocate an independent state of their own in Palestine.

The first clashes between Jews and Arabs and between Arabs and the British also began at this time. There were serious Arab riots in 1920 and 1921. After a lull, Arab riots, demonstrations, and terrorist attacks resumed in 1929. In 1936, a full-scale armed rebellion broke out that lasted for three years.

The initial riots and demonstrations were largely spontaneous. There was no leadership at the time that could negotiate with the

British over the conditions that had led to the disturbances. That was, again, attributable to the Palestinians' peculiar colonial status. The British refused to allow even a colonial parliament in which the Arabs could participate. Moreover, they encouraged rivalry between the two leading families, the Husaynis and Nashashibis, and between Christians (whom they appointed to the bulk of administrative positions) and Muslims. Almost by default, the movement for an Arab Palestine—initially led by Christians and Muslims—became increasingly identified with the more populous Muslims—and with a deeply flawed Muslim leader whom the British themselves had appointed.

In 1921, the British created a new post of grand mufti of Jerusalem to rule over the state's Muslims. Bypassing the recommendations of local clerics, the British appointed the young Haji Amin al-Husayni to the post, hoping that he would help them quell the rebellion against the Jews and themselves. For almost fifteen years, al-Husayni played along with the British. In the early 1930s, he helped undermine a secular nationalist party that had been formed to represent the Arabs of Palestine. But when the massive rebellion of 1936 broke out, al-Husayni, fearful of losing his support among Arabs, assumed leadership of it.

The clashes during the rebellion took place primarily between Arabs and the British, but they were intended to discourage the British from backing Zionism. The British attempted to co-opt the rebels by offering a compromise. A commission headed by Earl Peel recommended partitioning Palestine between a strip running up the coast and including the northern valleys that would be Jewish, a central area including Jerusalem and its immediate environs, that would remain under British control, and the rest of the country, including the Negev, that would be under Palestinian control. It was—viewed in retrospect—a very generous offer, and some Arab notables favored taking it. But the mufti, riding high in his new role as the leader of the Arab rebellion, and fearful of losing support from the fellaheen, refused even to meet with the Peel Commission.

The British subsequently brought in 25,000 additional troops to quash the rebellion. Over 5,000 Arabs were killed and 15,000 wounded during the revolt. Towns were razed, the Arab urban economy was wrecked, and what existed of a Palestinian leadership was killed, imprisoned, or exiled. The grand mufti himself was exiled. He fled initially to Lebanon and then to Iraq, but in 1941 moved to Berlin where he became a supporter of Hitler. He tried to return to Palestine after the war, but was blocked by the British. When the war broke out between the Arabs and Jews in 1947, he tried unsuccessfully to assume leadership from afar. Yet, during these years, there was no other Palestinian Arab who could speak or negotiate on behalf of the Palestinian Arabs. To all intents and purposes, the Palestinians were leaderless.

That accounts for what has to be the supreme irony of the interwar period. In 1939, in response to the rebellion and to the onset of World War II, the British issued a white paper that restricted Jewish immigration and land purchases and promised a binational state in ten years. There was considerable support for the White Paper among Arab notables, but the mufti, asserting his remaining authority from Beirut, made sure that the Arabs rejected any offer from the country that had exiled him. Instead, the main effect of the White Paper of 1939 was to infuriate Palestine's Jews who vowed to drive the British out and to achieve, finally, a Jewish Palestine. By 1939, most of what would occur after World War II and the defeat of Hitler—including the war against the British, the founding of Israel, and the frustration of Palestinian Arabs' hopes for a state of their own—had already been set in motion.

The Impact of Political Factions

In Palestine at the same time, there was a broad political division between the Jews in Israel that would endure well past Israel's founding. The majority—sometimes identified as Labor Zionists and led by David Ben-Gurion—favored the gradual establishment of a Jewish state in Mandate Palestine through immigration (which would create a Jewish majority) and, if necessary, through the transfer of Arabs into Transjordan or other neighboring countries. Ben-Gurion was willing to accept partition in 1937 and again in 1947, but only as a first step. "Erect a Jewish State at once, even if it is not in the whole land. The rest will come in the course of time. It must come," Ben-Gurion wrote his son in 1937.[8]

The minority—dubbed the "Revisionists" and led by Vladimir Jabotinsky and later Menachem Begin—went even further. They sought to "revise" the Balfour Declaration to include the East Bank of the Jordan as well as the West Bank. The Revisionists, who founded their own organization and armed groups in 1935, also favored forcibly seizing the land from the Arabs rather than waiting for a majority to be achieved through immigration. Relations between the Zionist groups remained hostile, but the British White Paper of 1939 and the Holocaust brought them together.

By restricting immigration, the White Paper of 1939 threatened the promise of a Jewish majority. In response, Ben-Gurion and the Zionist majority argued initially that it was necessary to drive the British out and establish a Jewish state in order to achieve a majority. By murdering six million European Jews, the Holocaust undermined the promise of an immediate Jewish majority even through open immigration, but the revelation of mass murder, and the presence of 250,000 Jews languishing after the war in displaced persons camps, legitimized Zionism internationally, especially in the United States, and lent added urgency to the Zionist cause in Palestine. It now became necessary and justifiable, as the Revisionists had argued, to create a Jewish state even before a majority had been assembled. In September 1946, the two wings of the Zionist movement took up arms to drive the British out of Palestine and establish a Jewish state.

The Jewish forces could not defeat the British, but by staging spectacular attacks (including the bombing of the King David Hotel by Begin's Irgun), they were able to tie down 100,000 British police and army at a time when the British economy, already burdened by wartime debt, was reeling under a recession. In February 1947, the British gave up not just Palestine, but many of their imperial responsibilities in the Mediterranean and the Middle East. They formally ceded their mandate for Palestine back to the newly established United Nations, leaving them to decide what to do with it. But, as the British recognized, they were in fact transferring outside responsibility for the region to the United States and to the Truman administration.

MILITARY IMPLICATIONS

During World War II, Franklin Roosevelt had tried to please both the Jews at home and the Arab states abroad, whose support the United States and Britain deemed essential for the war against Hitler. He invited Rabbis Stephen Wise and Abba Hillel Silver to the White House in March 1944 and authorized the two men to say that the administration backed a "Jewish national home." But one week before his death, Roosevelt also wrote Saudi King Abdul Aziz Ibn Saud, who had protested American support for a Jewish Palestine, promising that "no decision be taken with respect to the basic situation in that country without full consultation with both Arabs and Jews" and that the United States would take no action "which might prove hostile to the Arab people."[9]

*President Truman awarding Legion of Merit to Crown Prince Amir
Saud of Saudi Arabia, February 18, 1947. The prince also accepted a
similar award on behalf of his father, King Ibn Saud. The awards were
bestowed for the support the Saudis had provided the Allies in World
War II. (TL 63–1392–11)*

Truman's support for Zionism had also been equivocal. In 1939,
he had attacked the British White Paper in a speech on the Senate
floor, charging that "it made a scrap of paper out of Balfour's promise."[10] But in 1944, he had failed to support a Senate resolution in
favor of a Jewish commonwealth and unlimited immigration into
Palestine.[11] Soon after he became president, he was deeply moved by
revelations of the Nazi Holocaust and of the plight of the Jewish refugees in Europe, which led him to urge the British to remove the
restrictions on Jewish immigration, but did not lead him to favor a
Jewish state.

It was Truman's hope that if the British permitted the Jews to
emigrate, the Zionists in Palestine would cease to agitate for their
own state and accept British rule. In April 1946, he cheered the
report of an Anglo-American Committee of Inquiry that recommended the immediate transfer to Palestine of 100,000 refugees, but
also endorsed a Palestine "under international guarantees" that was
"neither a Jewish state nor an Arab state."[12] Even after Truman had
agreed to recognize the new state of Israel two years later, he told a

member of the committee that he still believed its earlier recommendation of a federated state was "the correct solution."[13]

Truman's reservations about a Jewish state stemmed in large part from arguments that State Department and Pentagon officials were making. These officials, who included Secretary of State George Marshall and Secretary of Defense James Forrestal, argued that by appearing to favor the Jews, the United States would alienate Arab states that were essential to the Cold War alliance against the Soviet Union. They also contended that by encouraging a Jewish state, the United States would unleash decades of war and create a state dependent on the United States for its survival.

If the United States were to make good on a commitment to Zionism, and to prevent a long-lasting conflict, State Department and Pentagon officials asserted, it would have to send troops into the region to prevent war between the Jews and the Arabs. In 1945, the State Department estimated that 400,000 troops would be needed to pacify the region—equal to almost the entire demobilized American army. That inflated figure was designed to scare Truman, and it clearly did. He announced that the United States had "no desire to send 500,000 American soldiers there to make peace in Palestine."[14]

In early 1948, when Truman was considering whether to recognize Israel, the Pentagon estimated that the United States would have to send at least 50,000 troops as part of a United Nations force to keep the Jews and Arabs apart. That was a considerably lower figure, but it loomed as large at the time because the United States was facing the possibility of war in Europe with the Soviet Union. The

President Truman flanked by Secretary of State Dean Acheson (left) and Secretary of Defense George C. Marshall (right), 1950. At the time of Truman's recognition of Israel, Marshall was Secretary of State and Acheson served as his deputy. (TL 60–42)

Pentagon intended their estimate to also discourage Truman from taking favorable action on the Jewish state.

Yet, in spite of being convinced by each succeeding argument—and voicing them at each turn, before and after he had made decisions—Truman steadily moved toward accepting the new state of Israel. In a speech the day after Yom Kippur in October 1946, he announced his support for a Jewish state. The next year, he threw American support behind the United Nations plan to partition Palestine into Jewish and Arab states, which the Arab nations rejected as being wildly unfair, and over which Palestinian Arabs threatened war. (Even though Jews made up a third of the population, they would receive 56 percent of the land.) And then, on May 14, 1948, against the advice of the State Department, Truman recognized the new State of Israel.

Why did Truman finally reject the advice of his foreign policy experts and, it would appear, his own considered judgments on what would be best? Truman would later deny it, but one reason seems to have been political pressure from American Zionists, who were able to reach Truman not only through organized groups, but through the president's White House staff and old personal friends. What was later called the pro-Israel lobby saw its birth during the Truman years.

PRESSURE FROM ZIONISTS

When Herzl first launched the Zionist movement in the 1890s, American Jews did not prove to be receptive. Their situation was different from that of their European counterparts. In the United States, where denominationalism prevailed, Jews had won recognition as a religious, rather than a national, group. They were subject to the same laws as other religious denominations. Accordingly, the Union of American Hebrew Congregations had passed a resolution in 1898 saying, "We are unalterably opposed to political Zionism. The Jews are not a nation, but a religious community."[15]

The first important American convert to Zionism was future Supreme Court judge Louis Brandeis, but for Brandeis, supporting Zionism meant supporting a haven in Palestine for European Jews who suffered from anti-Semitism. It did not mean encouraging Americans to emigrate. Said Brandeis in 1915, "Every American who aids in advancing the Jewish settlement in Palestine, though he feels that neither he nor his descendants will ever live there, will likewise be a better man and a better American for doing so."[16]

Maurice Bisgyer, Eddie Jacobson, and Frank Goldman holding pens presented to them by President Truman after he signed the document extending full diplomatic recognition to the government of Israel on January 31, 1949. Bisgyer was executive vice president of B'nai B'rith; Goldman was president of B'nai B'rith. (TL 2004–33)

Even in the mid-1930s, as word of Nazi anti-Semitism began to be heard, the Zionist Organization of America (ZOA) boasted only 50,000 members. The wealthiest and best-connected Jews belonged to the American Jewish Committee, which opposed Zionism. But World War II and the revelations about the Holocaust completely altered the political landscape. In 1943, the ZOA spun off the American Zionist Emergency Council (AZEC), chaired by Wise and Silver, to promote American support for a Jewish state. By 1945, the membership of American Zionist organizations was around 280,000. And the American Jewish Committee would go from being "non-Zionist" to finally, on the eve of the founding of Israel, "pro-Zionist."

The pressure from organized Zionist groups took the form of letter writing campaigns, demonstrations, and visits to the White House by group leaders. In September 1945, when Truman was wavering on whether to demand that Britain allow Jewish refugees to emigrate to Palestine, the AZEC held a demonstration at Madison Square Garden in New York and sent 200,000 telegrams to the White House. But the Zionist pressure worked best when it was tied to elections. In the 1940s, winning the Jewish vote was critical not only to winning elections in New York (the state with the most electoral votes and Jewish voters), but also in Ohio, Illinois, and Pennsylvania. In 1946, the AZEC urged Jews to vote as a bloc based on the administration's stand on a new Jewish state. This pressure was instrumental in getting Truman to give his "Yom Kippur speech."

Influential Jews, acting on their own or at the urging of the organized movement, were also able to sway Truman. Business executive Abraham Feinberg and other wealthy Jewish donors to Truman's campaigns took advantage of their access to the president to urge him, at critical junctures, to favor a Jewish state. Within the White House, Brandeis disciple David Niles worked closely with Wise at the AZEC and with Jewish Agency representative Eliahu Epstein to win Truman over. Another Brandeis disciple, Max Lowenthal, advised Truman's chief of staff, Clark Clifford, who himself became an important defender of the Zionist cause. And Truman's former army buddy and business partner, Eddie Jacobson, seems to have had a profound influence on Truman's decision to throw U.S. weight behind the United Nations vote for partition.

A MORAL IMPERATIVE

But there was another factor in Truman's decisions to back the formation of Israel that cannot be gleaned simply from what he said at the time. If one looks at the discussion that took place from April 1945 to May 1948, one finds that there is not a clear distinction to be made between the "rational" proposals of the State Department on geopolitical grounds and the "emotional" or "political" decisions that Truman finally made. If Truman's final decisions reflected domestic pressures, the State Department proposals seem to have been predicated on wishful thinking.

The State Department and the Pentagon were certainly more right than wrong about the regional consequences of Israel's becoming a state. They were also on firm ground in advising Truman not to appear to take one side against another. Being "evenhanded" would later be condemned by the pro-Israel lobby, but it represented the only approach that could conceivably lead to reconciliation between the warring parties. Where the State Department and the Pentagon departed from reality was in their proposals about how to prevent the disastrous consequences of an Arab-Israeli war.

In Truman's first years in office, the State Department and the Pentagon urged him to prop up British control over Palestine, but Britain was in no position to maintain its older empire, whether in

South Asia or the Near East. And sure enough, Britain finally gave up in February 1947. With Britain out of the picture, State Department officials proposed an "international trusteeship" for Palestine that would result either in a binational nation or an amicable agreement on partition between the Jews and Arabs. But with the United Nations still an infant organization lacking an organized army, such an international trusteeship would not have stemmed the rush to statehood by the Jews or to war by the Arabs. It was an empty formulation.

By the same token, Truman's own misgivings about his decisions—his repeated assertions that the Anglo-American Commission's proposal of a federated Palestine made the most sense—were largely based on an unwillingness to acknowledge the reality on the ground in Palestine. It was not a case of narrow politics versus reasoned geopolitics, but politics versus wishful thinking. It does not speak well of Truman, who was known for his decisiveness in prosecuting the Cold War, that he had difficulty making up his mind and was finally swayed by political pressure; but it would not have spoken well of him to have held out for a binational or a federated Palestine, especially after the United Nations had ruled in favor of partition.

In truth, Truman had no good options. The only remotely feasible alternative for Truman and the State Department was to back up the original partition of November 1947 with a powerful UN peacekeeping force that included a substantial American contingent. Such a force might have prevented war from breaking out and, if combined with development aid, given the Palestinians the opportunity to create a state of their own. But the administration was not ready to make that kind of commitment. It was not a sufficiently high priority. In 1948 Truman and his foreign policy officials were focused almost entirely on the Soviet threat in Europe. And some of these officials were worried—and with good reason—that even if the United States plunged troops into Palestine, it would not do any good. Yet, without a willingness to use American power to affect the region, American policy was feckless.

For the remainder of his term in office, Truman's diplomacy in the region proved to be either ineffective or overly solicitous of Israeli wishes. Truman was committed in principle to an evenhanded policy that would retain the allegiance of Arab states, but in practice he ended up doing the bidding of the Israelis and their supporters in the United States. In the fall of 1948, Truman initially endorsed a UN peace plan to end the war, but under intense political pressure during the last two months of the presidential campaign, he reneged. After he had won the election, he tried to revive American support for the plan, but Israeli advances on the ground had already rendered it moot. In the subsequent negotiations over what to do about the 700,000 Arab refugees created by the war, Truman initially backed a State Department plan to threaten Israel with a loss of loan money unless it accepted refugees, but once again backed down under pressure.

Having failed to achieve a peace agreement between the Israelis and Arabs, the Truman administration signed a tripartite agreement with Britain and France pledging to levy sanctions against any nation that violated the 1948 armistice lines. But this agreement, like the Kellogg-Briand Pact that the United States, Germany, Japan, and other nations signed in 1928 renouncing war, proved barely worth the paper it was printed on. Six years later, the British, French, and Israelis ignored it when they invaded Egypt and seized control of the Suez Canal.

Recapitulation

In the sixty years since Truman recognized Israel, the Jewish state has grown and prospered. It has also served as a haven for persecuted Jews from Arab countries and the Soviet Union. As Weizmann had promised, it has introduced Western-style capitalism and politics into the Middle East. But there is, of course, another side to this story. The Jewish settlement of Palestine, as Jabotinsky was one of the first to note, had to come into conflict with the national aspirations of the Arabs who already lived there. This conflict could have been foreseen as early as 1920, when the first riots took place in Jerusalem. And in the last sixty years, the clash over the land once called Palestine has continued and has expanded.

What is disturbing about this history is that the pattern of conflict and the behavior of the principal actors have not changed substantially in the last sixty, or in some cases, one hundred years. The present has recapitulated the past. The Palestinians, for example, have continued to be plagued by poor leadership and by sectarian disunity. That does not date from the founding of Hamas, but from the time of the British Mandate. Any vestige of leadership the rebellion of 1936–39 had failed to destroy was destroyed in the wars of 1947 and 1948. And the people themselves were dispersed. About 700,000 refugees lived in camps in Gaza, Jordan, Syria, and Lebanon. What remained of Arab Palestine after 1948 was controlled by Jordan, which forbade the use of the term "Palestine" in official documents. Palestinian politics, to the extent they existed, were under the control of the Arab states in the region, who were intent (as they were in the 1948 war) on using the Palestinians to advance their own fractious agendas.

In 1964, with the backing of these states, the Palestine Liberation Organization (PLO) was founded under the leadership of Yasser Arafat and the Fatah organization. The PLO, too, was dependent on its state sponsors, and in 1978, under the influence of Syria and Iraq, it refused to alter its charter calling for Israel's destruction (even though the Palestinian leadership had privately shifted to a two-state solution) and blocked participation by local Palestinians in the Camp David talks. As a result, it missed a chance to secure a degree of self-rule and to impose a barrier on settlements in the West Bank and Gaza before they began in earnest.

Arafat himself was the heir to the mufti; he was a brilliant organizer who at crucial times sacrificed the welfare of his people to the perpetuation of his power. Arafat was effective in uniting the PLO as an outside force, but like the mufti, he proved incapable of creating a structure of government for the Palestinians. After the Oslo talks in 1993—where he and the PLO shoved aside the Palestinians' indigenous leadership—Arafat set up a corrupt patronage regime. In 2000 at Camp David, he turned down a generous offer from the Israelis out of fear of losing control of Palestinian militants, even though the Israeli offer would likely have won the support of most Palestinians in the West Bank and Gaza. And things have not improved with Arafat's demise. The current Palestinian leadership struggle between Hamas and Fatah is reminiscent of the division between the Husaynis and Nashashibis, but it makes the older rivalry look like friendly jousting.

NECESSARY MEANS

The Israelis concluded from their success at war in 1947 and 1948 that they could achieve security through military means. Nahum Goldmann, a leader of the Zionist movement, wrote afterwards of the war, "It seemed to show the advantages of direct action over negotiation and diplomacy. The victory offered such a glorious contrast to the centuries of persecution and humiliation, of adaptation and compromise, that it seemed to indicate the only direction that could be taken from then on. To brook nothing, tolerate no attack, cut through Gordian knots, and shape history by creating facts seemed so simple, so compelling, so satisfying that it became Israel's policy in its conduct with the Arab world."[17]

Israel would apply this lesson again and again. In the Suez invasion of 1956, the Six-Day War of 1967, and the subsequent war of attrition, they tried to undermine Gamal Abdel Nasser's rule in Egypt. In the invasion of Lebanon in 1982, they wanted to rid Israel of the threat from Arafat and the PLO. In the war with Lebanon in 2006, they tried to eliminate Hezbollah. And in the countless brutal reprisals—which invariably outdid the mayhem and killing that they were in response to—they tried to intimidate the rebellious Palestinians. Some of these attacks were temporarily successful, but as a whole, they have perpetuated the Israelis' war with the Arabs.

Most recently, Israel Prime Minister Ariel Sharon responded to the second intifada (2001–2006) by resuming the occupation of the West Bank and seeking to destroy the Palestinian Authority. While Palestinian attacks killed about a thousand Israelis, Israelis in turn killed over four thousand Palestinians. Sharon modeled his strategy on the British suppression of the Arab revolt of 1936–39.[18] Arafat's government virtually ceased to operate, but it did not give way to a moderate and conciliatory Palestinian leadership. Instead, it was replaced by the radical Islamic organization Hamas that was committed to replacing Israel with an Arab-dominated Palestine.

Historically, the Jews of Palestine had failed to take the Palestinian demands for self-determination seriously. The first waves of Jewish settlers either ignored or denigrated the rights of the Arabs who already lived there. A favorite saying was Israel Zangwill's description of Palestine as "A land without a people for a people without a land."[19] Even after the 1936–39 rebellion, those leaders who recognized that the Arabs had a claim upon the same lands accorded the Jews a vastly superior claim, especially after the Holocaust. On the eve of the new state, Werner Senator, an official of the Jewish Agency, said: "If I weigh the catastrophe of five million Jews against the transfer of one million Arabs, then with a clean and easy conscience I can state that even more drastic acts are permissible."[20]

That view of the Palestinian Arabs as having a lesser claim has persisted. In 1969, Israeli Prime Minister Golda Meir would insist to London's *Times* that "there was no such thing as Palestinians."[21] That attitude would buttress the continuing belief that Israel had a right to all of Mandate Palestine. Even today, an Israeli political party that is part of the government openly advocates transferring Palestinians out of the West Bank to Jordan. If anything, these sentiments have been reinforced by the increasingly desperate and self-destructive means that the Palestinians have used to protest their subjugation.

After the 1948 war, in which the Israelis succeeded in conquering 78 percent of Mandate Palestine, many of the country's leaders did put aside, for the time being, their dreams of placing all of Palestine, including East Jerusalem, under Jewish rule. But as Gershom Gorenberg has shown in *The Accidental Empire,* this vision persisted among left-wing and right-wing intellectuals and party leaders.[22]

Revisionism itself survived the 1948 war. Begin formed the Herut party, which later became the central component of the Likud party. Israel's success in the Six-Day War rekindled the dreams of "greater Israel" and gave birth to the settler movement, which gained momentum after Begin's Likud party came to power in the 1977 elections. Israel's Jews, who had fled other countries to escape oppression as a national minority, now ruled over the Palestinians in the West Bank and Gaza. Long accused by Arabs of being an arm of Western colonialism in the region, Israel became a colonial power in its own right. That precluded any reconciliation with Palestinian Arabs.

PERSISTENT FAILURES

Over the decades since Truman left office, American diplomacy has suffered from many of the same shortcomings in Middle East policy as were present during Truman's administration. It has often been paralyzed by divisions between supporters of Israel in the White House and Congress and the "Arabists" of the State Department. While the State Department urged that policy be "evenhanded" or that the United States act as an "honest broker," the White House and Congress have often (although not always) insisted the United States act as a "friend" of Israel.[23] That put several administrations in the position of encouraging tendencies in Israeli policy that made reconciliation in the region less likely.

During Ronald Reagan's first term, he repudiated American support for UN Resolution 242 (which called on Israel to return to its 1967 boundaries) and rejected the Carter administration's charge that Israel's settlements were illegal. At a press conference in February 1981, Reagan declared that the West Bank settlements were "not illegal."[24] The next year, Reagan and his secretary of state, Alexander Haig, failed to prevent Israel from invading Lebanon. Reagan and his new secretary of state, George Shultz, eventually turned against the Israeli invasion, but only after it—and America's association with it—had sparked the beginning of terrorist attacks against Americans in the region.

George W. Bush's foreign policies provide the best example of how the United States has sometimes encouraged Israel's worst tendencies. Bush abandoned the peace process that his predecessor Bill Clinton had initiated (the very term "peace process" was banished from the administration lexicon) and backed the attempt by Israeli Prime Minister Ariel Sharon to destroy the Palestinian Authority and drive Arafat from office. Like Sharon, he hoped that more moderate leadership would emerge from the crushed rebellion.

After it was clear that the war would not bring peace, Bush insisted that the Palestinians hold elections so that Israel and the United States would have an administration to negotiate with, while conceding to Sharon that the United States would no longer demand that Israel dismantle its largest settlements. Predictably, Hamas won the election. Bush then refused even to talk to the Hamas officials (even though the United States maintains diplomatic relations with other governments hostile to Israel) and approved of Israeli confiscation of Palestinian tax revenues upon which any Palestinian government relies. Later, Bush also quietly backed Israel's attempt to drive Hezbollah out of Lebanon and discouraged the Israeli government from negotiating with Syria. When Bush leaves office, he will leave Israeli-Palestinian relations in a shambles.

Those administrations that have sought to be "evenhanded" have often been stymied either by the domestic lobby or by Arab or Israeli intransigence. The Kennedy administration tried and failed to win an Israeli compromise on admitting refugees; Carter was stiffed by the Syrians; the Reagan administration, after its disastrous intervention in Lebanon, attempted unsuccessfully to win Israeli support for a peace plan. Clinton, of course, met rejection from Arafat. In most of these instances, the administration could have gone further and applied the leverage the United States has on Israel or on American Arab allies, but was reluctant to do so. One reason was the domestic repercussions. When George H. W. Bush's administration threatened to withhold loans until Israel participated in the Madrid peace conference, it prompted outcry from the Israelis and from their supporters in the United States. Bush persisted, and got the Israelis to participate, but he paid for his persistence during the 1992 election—a lesson probably not lost on his oldest son.

The irony, of course, was that when American administrations attempted to be evenhanded, that strategy benefited the Israelis more than when they tried to be "friends." George H. W. Bush's insistence on Israel's participation in Madrid led to the Oslo negotiations and to eight years of relative peace and prosperity. In contrast, Reagan's encouragement of settlements and initial acquiescence in the invasion of Lebanon led to a nightmare for Israel in Lebanon and to the first intifada. Equally, George W. Bush's tilt to Israel led to the election of Hamas. In others words, American policy, by tilting toward Israel in these years, led to a situation that was detrimental to the United States and Israel and the Palestinians. In the Truman years, the initial tilt to Israel was by default, and almost inadvertence—Truman and the State Department did not have a clear alternative—but what was inadvertent became deliberate and resulted in policies that made peace between Israel and the Arabs difficult, if not impossible

LESSONS NOT LEARNED

It was not, strictly speaking, inevitable that the conflict that began in Jerusalem at the turn of the last century should continue into this new century. History does not work that way. Sometimes peoples do learn from the past, as France and Germany learned from the experience of four hundred years of war, culminating in two world wars. But it does usually take a cataclysm of this kind to force nations to change their historic ways. Otherwise, they seem to repeat their errors and misconceptions. This is what, sadly, has happened to the Jews and Arabs of the former Palestine and to American policy in that region.

There have, of course, been moments of lucidity when the actors seemed to recognize that they were reading from a script that, if not significantly altered, would lead to a very unhappy ending. But those moments seem to have passed; Yitzhak Rabin gave way to Benyamin Netanyahu, Bill Clinton to George W. Bush, and the Palestinian moderates to Hamas. One hopes that recounting what happened—as the contributors to this book do—will help the principal actors become aware of their destructive patterns and change course without having to suffer a catastrophe. But just as conflict and failure have not been inevitable, neither is there any guarantee of peace and reconciliation. It may be many decades before an administration is able to answer Truman's $64 question.

Notes

[1] *Foreign Relations of the United States, 1945*. Vol. 8, *The Near East and Africa* (Washington, DC: U.S. Government Printing Office, 1969), 13–18.

[2] Some authors have combined two or more of these answers to why the Arab-Israeli conflict has persisted, but at the risk of oversimplifying, one can put Efraim Karsh, Michael Oren, Joan Peters, and Alan Dershowitz in the first camp; some of Israel's "new historians" (including Avi Shlaim, Ilan Pappe, and Tom Segev) and Edward Said in the second; and George Ball and Stephen Green in the third. The characterization of Palestinians as "extremists" is from Efraim Karsh, *Fabricating Israeli History* (London: Frank Cass, 2000), 37. That of the Israelis as "victims" become victimizers can be found in Edward Said, "The Burdens of Interpretation and the Question of Palestine," *Journal of Palestine Studies* (Autumn 1986): 33.

[3] Margaret Macmillan, *Paris 1919: Six Months That Changed the World* (New York: Random House, 2002), 416.

[4] Walter Laqueur and Barry Rubin, eds., *The Israel-Arab Reader* (New York: Penguin, 1991), 16.

[5] "Palestine Mandate in Complete Text," *New York Times*, February 28, 1921, 6.

[6] Tom Segev, *One Palestine, Complete* (New York: Little Brown, 2000), 45.

[7] See Rashid Khalidi, *The Iron Cage:The Story of the Palestinian Struggle for Statehood* (Boston: Beacon Press, 2006).

[8] Avi Shlaim, *The Iron Wall: Israel and the Arab World* (New York: W. W. Norton, 2001), 21.

[9] *Foreign Relations of the United States, 1945*. Vol. 8, *The Near East and Africa*, 698.

[10] Peter Grose, *Israel in the Mind of America* (New York: Alfred A. Knopf, 1983), 189.

[11] Michael J. Cohen, *Truman and Israel* (Berkeley: University of California Press, 1990), 45.

[12] Charles L. Geddes, ed., *A Documentary History of the Arab-Israeli Conflict* (New York: Greenwood Publishing, 1991), 218.

[13] Cohen, *Truman and Israel,* 222.

[14] Harry S. Truman, *Public Papers of the President, 1945–53* (Washington, DC: U.S. Government Printing Office, 1961), 1945:228.

[15] Jonathan Sarna, *American Judaism* (New Haven: Yale University Press, 2004), 202.

[16] Edward Tivnan, *The Lobby: Jewish Political Power and American Foreign Policy* (New York: Simon and Schuster, 1987), 17.

[17] Shlaim, *The Iron Wall*, 40.

[18] Ari Shavit, "The General," *The New Yorker*, January 23, 2006, 55–56. Shavit wrote, Sharon "showed me the book he was reading: it was about the Arab Revolt of 1936–39. He said that what interested him was the way the rebellion had ultimately collapsed, causing a disintegration of Palestinian society. He clearly saw a certain similarity between the revolt of the 1930s and the intifada that began in 2000. In time, it became evident that the strategic plan that Sharon was considering involved bringing the Palestinians to a point of political chaos and then luring them into a partial agreement on Israel's terms—one that would not require evacuation of major settlements in the West Bank and a return to the pre-1967 borders."

[19] Shlomo Ben-Ami, *Scars of War, Wounds of Prosperity: The Israeli-Arab Tragedy* (New York: Oxford University Press, 2006), 4.

[20] Ben-Ami, *Scars of War,* 29.

[21] "Interview with Frank Giles," London's *Sunday Times,* June 15, 1969.

[22]Gershom Gorenberg, *The Accidental Empire* (New York: Times Books/Henry Holt, 2006), chaps. 1 and 2.

[23]See William B. Quandt, *Peace Process* (Washington, DC: Brookings/University of California, 2005), 59–62.

[24]"Excerpts from Interview with President Reagan Conducted by Five Reporters," *New York Times,* February 2, 1981.

Harry S. Truman, Jews, and the Recognition of Israel

HARRY S. TRUMAN AND JEWISH REFUGEES

Alan L. Berger

President Truman, whom Robert J. Donovan once described as "the most stubborn of Missouri mules," left a profound legacy for all Americans. But for American Jews, his actions in office had special resonance on two vital issues. In addition to admitting Jewish displaced persons to the United States after the war, the president granted American diplomatic recognition to the newly emergent State of Israel just eleven minutes after the state was formally declared. Despite the opposition of his distinguished secretary of state, General George C. Marshall, whom Truman greatly admired, and the reluctance of most of the president's other key advisors, Truman overruled the opponents within his administration who feared the creation of the modern Jewish state. Israel, they argued, would be inimical to America's interests in terms of national security; in particular, access to oil reserves in the Arab states surrounding Israel. There were also concerns that recognition of Israel would complicate international relations and give the Soviet Union entry to the Middle East.

The displaced persons, or DPs (as they were called), issue and recognition of Israel are intimately related. However, Truman's actions and his motives in making decisions on these two issues are clouded in the seemingly contradictory words of the president and the actions of the American government concerning Jews and immigration. In a 1943 speech delivered at the Chicago United Rally to Demand Rescue of Doomed Jews, the then Senator Harry S. Truman, expressed his outrage at what was taking place in Nazi-occupied Europe. After first attesting that "the history of America in its fight for freedom and the history of the Jews of America are one and the same," he noted that National Socialism intended "the systematic slaughter throughout all of Europe, not only of the Jews but of vast numbers of other innocent peoples." Truman then issued a call to action. "We must," he asserted, "do all that is humanly possible to provide a haven and place of safety for all those who can be grasped from the hands of the Nazi butchers."[1] The subsequent tale of America and the displaced persons provides a revealing look at Truman, Congress, and American anti-Semitism—both during and immediately following the Holocaust.

Senator Truman's remarks echoed—in tone if not circumstance—George Washington's 1783 speech in New York. At that time, President Washington observed:

> The bosom of America is open to receive not only the opulent and respectable stranger, but the oppressed and persecuted of all nations and religions; whom we shall welcome to a participation of all our rights and privileges, if by decency and propriety of conduct they appear to merit the enjoyment.[2]

Truman, like his eighteenth-century predecessor, led a country that had both noble principles and a deeply rooted nativism. To put the matter bluntly, general acceptance by Americans of DPs was one thing, Jewish DPs were quite another matter. While I am not an expert in psychohistory, nor, for that matter, do I claim credentials as an historian, I think it significant to note that Truman was an avid reader who claimed to have "read the Bible through many times,"[3] and his profound personal convictions, not infrequently at odds with diplomatic and political considerations, favored the admission of Jewish refugees to America on humanitarian grounds.

It is important to recall two important facts when considering the DP issue at the end of World War II. First, the Jews were singled out in the Holocaust in an unprecedented manner. They were not political prisoners, dissidents, POWs, saboteurs, or armed members of an enemy force bent on conquering Germany. Their "crime" consisted in having been born. In the words of Elie Wiesel, "while not all victims were Jews, all Jews were victims."[4] Related to this is the fact that the Holocaust, for Jews, did not end in 1945. The trauma continued in several ways; Jewish prisoners were frequently locked in DP camps with their former tormentors, and some Jews in the camps were actually given Nazi uniforms to wear. In addition, German personnel, many of whom were deeply anti-Semitic, were often put in positions of authority by United States military commanders at the end of the war. The effects of these traumatic experiences on Jewish survivors are only now beginning to be recognized and commented on by historians. Moreover, anti-Semitic attitudes in America seemed to grow during the war years.

Second, compounding the trauma for Jewish DPs was the fact that certain high-ranking American military personnel were themselves anti-Semites. One thinks here of General George S. Patton, commander of the Third Army in southern Germany, an area that contained most of the DPs in the American zone. In a September 15, 1945, diary entry, Patton wrote that others "believe that the displaced person is a human being, which he is not, and this applies particularly to the Jews who are lower than animals." Furthermore, there existed a belief that the DPs had to be treated as prisoners or else they would leave the camps, "spread over the country like locusts, and would eventually have to be rounded up after quite a few of them had been shot and quite a few Germans murdered and pillaged."[5] Robert Ross, writing in *So It Was True*, is absolutely correct in observing: "The last chapter in the Nazi persecution of the Jews was written in the displaced-person camps and in the emigration of survivors during the years after the war in Europe."[6]

President Truman faced considerable pressure on the matter of Jewish displaced persons. However, the majority of the DPs were not Jewish, and the Anglo-American Commission of Inquiry and the Morrison-Grady Plan concerning the emigration of 100,000 Jews to Palestine set off a political firestorm. Zionist, and even non-Zionist, Jews in America bitterly attacked the proposal, which would have in effect given the Arabs a veto over Jewish emigration. Jewish political pressure was intense and sometimes counterproductive. At one point, Truman was so angry and frustrated at what he perceived as his harassment by Jewish leaders on this matter that he said during a cabinet meeting, "Jesus Christ couldn't please them when he was here on earth, so how could anyone expect that I would have any luck."[7] Clearly, this statement reflected Truman's sense of exasperation at the time. It also mirrored the type of religio-cultural anti-Semitism typical of the midwestern America in which the president had been raised.

A more comprehensive portrait of the president's personal feelings on the matter of Jewish emigration emerges from other sources. On November 24, 1945, he wrote, but never mailed, a letter to Minnesota Senator Joseph H. Ball, in which he stated, "What I am trying to do is make the whole world safe for the Jews. Therefore, I don't feel like going to war for Palestine."[8] Truman's meeting near the end of that year with Chaim Weizmann, subsequently the Jewish state's first president, favorably influenced him. There is considerable irony in the attraction the two men felt for each other. Weizmann was an intellectual, a university professor, a distinguished scientist, and a secular Jew. Truman was a Missouri Baptist who never attended college and who grew up in a time and place where anti-Semitism was normal; his mother-in-law, Madge Wallace, was a confirmed anti-Semite. Yet, the two men clearly respected each other.

Two other personal sources must be considered. One is Eddie Jacobson, Truman's former partner in a failed haberdashery store. Certainly they constituted one of history's most notable odd couples—Jacobson was the Brooklyn-born son of an Orthodox Jewish family who moved to Kansas when he was two years old. Jacobson had an extraordinary influence on Truman. The two men were close friends throughout their adult lives. Having first met in the Missouri National Guard, they served together in France during World War I, and later opened a famously unsuccessful haberdashery in Kansas City. In the months prior to Truman's recognition of Israel, Jacobson

Truman walking with Eddie Jacobson in Kansas City, May 17, 1953. (TL 75–497)

was a frequent visitor to the White House. At one point, before meeting Weizmann, Truman refused to see any Jewish representative.
Jacobson intervened, flattering and cajoling Truman. Exhausted, or
perhaps persuaded, the president told his longtime friend, "All right,
you bald-headed SOB, I'll see Weizmann."[9] Jacobson's influence on
Truman concerning Jewish matters is immeasurable. In addition to
Jacobson, David Niles, a holdover from the Roosevelt administration,
had great sympathy for Zionism and the cause of Jewish emigration.
He constantly articulated the Jewish cause to Truman and served as a
conduit for Jewish leaders who wished to give pertinent messages to
the president.

Alarmed by reports from and about the DP camps, Truman
authorized the mission of Earl G. Harrison, dean of the Law School
at the University of Pennsylvania, to assess the conditions and needs
of the displaced persons with particular reference to the Jewish refugees who might be stateless or nonrepatriable. Harrison's report was
sharply critical of the Allies' treatment of Jewish survivors and
called for major policy changes toward the Jewish remnant in
Europe. Truman received Harrison's report, perhaps the most influential of the DP period as it captured the president's attention, in
August 1945. Among Harrison's recommendations was the following observation: "Refusal to recognize the Jews as such has the
effect...of closing one's eyes to their former and more barbaric persecution, which has already made them a separate group with greater
needs." The report also noted the need for "promptly developing a
plan to get out of Germany and Austria as many as possible of those
who wish it." Harrison's report included the ominous reflection that
currently "we appear to be treating the Jews as the Nazis treated
them except that we do not exterminate them." While this may have
been an exaggeration, Harrison was not exaggerating when he
observed, "They are in concentration camps in large numbers under
our military guard instead of S.S. troops." The report's author concludes this section by asking the moral question, a query the Allies
never bothered to ask when it came to the treatment of Europe's
Jews at the close of World War II. "One is led to wonder," writes
Harrison, "whether the German people, seeing this, are not suppos-
ing that we are following or at least condoning Nazi policy."[10]

Within months of receiving Harrison's report, Truman issued a
directive on December 22, 1945, which began a sea change in American immigration policy. The directive stated that, within the existing quota system for Eastern Europe, preference should be given to

those who were persecuted people. Clearly Truman believed that this would be at least a small step in correcting the obscenity of allowing Nazis and their supporters into America while keeping the Jews incarcerated in camps under horrendous conditions. Unfortunately, and much to Truman's displeasure, the Displaced Persons Act of 1948 was riddled with restrictions that made it all but certain that only a very few of the Jewish displaced persons would find refuge in America. A 1950 Displaced Persons Act finally eliminated the discriminating features.

Frustrated with the anti-immigrant mood of Congress, Truman sought to circumvent congressional mischief by appointing liberals to the Displaced Persons Commission mandated in the 1948 Act. The commission began operating formally on August 27, 1948, and continued for the next four years. Under its auspices, nearly 340,000 DPs were resettled in America. Perhaps unwittingly, anticipating the appearance in 1955 of Will Herberg's classic study *Protestant, Catholic, Jew*, President Truman appointed as chair of the commission Ugo Carusi, a Protestant, who had formerly been United States Commissioner of Immigration; the other two members were Edward M. O'Connor of the National Catholic Welfare Conference and Harry N. Rosenfield, the Jewish member, who had served as an American delegate to UNESCO. The fact that Truman understood that a religious balance on the commission was necessary implicitly speaks to the changing attitude of America toward Jews and Judaism.

From the beginning, the Displaced Persons Commission followed one principle: get the DPs out of the assembly centers and "get them on the boats." Leonard Dinnerstein notes that this policy put the commission in direct conflict with State Department consulates and the Immigration and Naturalization Service bureaucrats "accustomed to finding reasons to exclude prospective immigrants."[11] Likewise, the commission's humane stance on immigration put it in direct conflict with the restrictive and shortsighted provisions of the McCarren-Walter Bill passed in 1952. Truman referred to this as the "terrible McCarren-Walter Bill," which "was nothing in the world but approval of all the mistakes the State and Justice have made in the last ten years in the administration of the immigration laws."[12] This legislation passed only after Truman's veto was overridden.

Truman's attitude towards Jews and other ethnic and racial groups is a complex topic. Clearly, Truman's views evolved over time as he experienced a wider world than he had known as a young man in small-town Missouri. Yet Harry S. Truman was very much a man of his times. He was highly opinionated and lacked the sophistication that a higher education might have provided.[13] He was not above giving voice to disparaging statements about Jews and some of their leaders. Indeed, he was fond of making disparaging statements about all those with whom he disagreed—including the music critic who panned his daughter's performance. He could also display great disdain for diplomatic niceties. Abba Eban recalls presenting his credentials as ambassador of Israel to the United States. Truman, writes Eban, "snatched the documents from my hand and said, 'Let's cut out the crap and have a real talk.'"[14]

On the other hand, Truman was much more than a man of his times. On the important issues, such as recognition of Israel and the immigration of refugees, desegregating the armed forces, and attempting to mainstream Native Americans into society, he appeared more like Reinhold Niebuhr's *Moral Man in an Immoral Society: A Study in Ethics and Politics.* Niebuhr contrasts the moral inferiority of groups with the moral standards of individuals. Inevitably, the conflict between the two results is a compromising of the moral standards of the individual. At least one reason that Truman's presidency is cited as a beacon of morality is that many of Truman's policies seem to contradict Niebuhr's well-argued attestation.

In the president's diary entry for April 15, 1952, he recalled the advice offered by two congressional committee chairmen (one of whom was Richard Russell from the state of Georgia) who reported to him, upon their return from the DP camps in Germany, that "we already had enough 'furriners' and needed no more!" Truman wrote that he responded by reminding the two that "displaced persons made this great nation what it is."[15] Originally, the president envisioned that 400,000 DPs would be admitted by the United States, as well as by South America and the British Commonwealth countries. The United States came closest to achieving that goal, taking in 339,000. Truman ends this entry by writing: "I hope that we will agree to 300,000 more. They are fine people and may be an addition to our bloodstream that we need right now."[16]

Truman proved to be a strong leader with personal beliefs and convictions that led him to act against the grain on a number of key policy issues. Nowhere is personal conviction more evident than in Truman's actions on displaced persons and the treatment of Jews. In neither case did Truman follow a route that was politically expedient. Most appropriately, Truman's commitment to personal responsibility was prominently displayed on his White House desk, "The Buck Stops Here."

Notes

[1] Harry S. Truman, Speech delivered at Chicago Stadium, Chicago, Illinois. 1943, April 14, United Rally to Demand Rescue of Doomed Jews, Chicago, IL, Press Release File, Speech Files, Papers as U.S. Senator and Vice President, Harry S. Truman Papers, Truman Library. I am grateful to Liz Safly of the Truman Library for her assistance in bringing this and other documents to my attention. I also wish to thank Bernard Smith for his careful reading of an earlier draft and for his suggestions.

[2] George Washington, quoted in the frontispiece of *Whom We Shall Welcome: Report of the President's Commission on Immigration and Naturalization* (Washington, DC: Superintendent of Documents, 1953).

[3] Harry S. Truman to Orville L. Freeman, February 7, 1958. In *Off the Record: The Private Papers of Harry S. Truman,* edited by Robert Ferrell (Columbia: University of Missouri Press, 1980), 355.

[4] Elie Wiesel, *Against Silence: The Voice and Vision of Elie Wiesel* (New York: Holocaust Library, 1985), 3:172.

[5] Quoted in Leonard Dinnerstein, *America and the Survivors of the Holocaust* (New York: Columbia University Press, 1982), 17

[6] Dinnerstein, *America and the Survivors,* frontispiece.

[7] Truman at a cabinet meeting, July 30, 1946. Cited by Robert J. Donovan, *Conflict and Crisis: The Presidency of Harry S. Truman 1945–1948* (New York: Norton, 1977), 319.

[8] Donovan, *Conflict and Crisis*, 315.

[9] Edward Jacobson to Joseph Cohn, April 1, 1952. Copies in the Weizmann Archives, Truman Library.

[10] Report of Earl G. Harrison, August 1945, Papers of Harry S. Truman, Official File 127, Truman Library.

[11] Dinnerstein, *America and the Survivors*, 184.

[12] Ferrell, *Off the Record*, 258.

[13] Jews appear to have played a significant role in Truman's personal and political life. Ted Marks, a tailor born in a Jewish section of Liverpool, was the best man at Truman's wedding; Milton Kayle, a Harvard-trained lawyer from New York, served as one of the president's speechwriters; and Judge and Mrs. Samuel I. Rosenman accompanied Harry and Bess Truman on their voyage to France. President Truman considered the judge "absolutely loyal and trustworthy" and "one of the ablest [judges] in Washington, keen mind, a lucid pen..."; Ferrell, *Off the Record*, 46, 350. I am grateful to Robert Watson for initial discussion on this matter.

[14] Abba Eban, "My First Forty-five Minutes with Harry S. Truman," in Larry S. Hackman, ed., *Harry S. Truman and the Recognition of Israel* (Independence, MO: Harry S. Truman Library, 1998). This essay is reprinted in this volume.

[15] Diary entry, April 15, 1952. In Ferrell, *Off the Record*, 248.

[16] Diary entry, April 15, 1952. In Ferrell, *Off the Record*, 248.

TRUMAN'S 1947 "ANTI-SEMITIC" DIARY ENTRY

Bruce S. Warshal

In July of 2003, the Harry S. Truman Library made public a hitherto unknown small diary written by President Truman during 1947. This amazing document had rested unnoticed on a shelf in the stacks of the library for decades in the covers of a booklet listing New York real estate agents and providing pages for daily entries of appointments and transactions. In that "1947 Diary" was a highly critical statement concerning Jews.

On July 21 of that year, after a ten-minute conversation with former treasury secretary Henry Morgenthau, in which the Jewish

The cover of a 1947 diary, bearing the title "1947 Diary and Manual of the Real Estate Board of New York, Inc.," that was sent to President Truman by Matthew G. Ely, the board's president in late 1946. Rose Conway, Truman's personal secretary, acknowledged the gift on December 27 and put the diary book "in the President's desk in office." A slip of paper interleaved in the diary book when it was discovered at the Truman Library in 2003, marked "President's Study," suggests that Truman used it in his oval study in the White House Residence. (1947, Diaries File, President's Secretary's File, Harry S. Truman Papers, Truman Library)

former treasury secretary pressured Truman on behalf of Jewish refugees attempting to enter Palestine, Truman wrote: "He'd no business, whatever to call me. The Jews have no sense of proportion nor do they have any judgment on world affairs." Truman then ranted:

> The Jews, I find, are very, very selfish. They care not how many Estonians, Latvians, Finns, Poles, Yugoslavs or Greeks get murdered or mistreated as D[isplaced] P[ersons] as long as the Jews get special treatment. Yet when they have power, physical, financial or political neither Hitler nor Stalin has anything on them for cruelty or mistreatment to the underdog. Put an underdog on top and it makes no difference whether his name is Russian, Jewish, Negro, Management, Labor, Mormon, Baptist he goes haywire. I've found very few who remember their past condition, when prosperity comes.[1]

Is this the same man who, just ten months later, gave de facto recognition to the State of Israel merely eleven minutes after its birth? Could Harry Truman have been a closet anti-Semite? I personally doubt it and, to date, Jewish reaction has been muted. However, *Washington Post* columnist Richard Cohen declared he "would have decked him,"[2] and *New York Times* columnist William Safire smugly declared that this was "more dismaying" than Nixon's slurs about Jews on his famous White House tapes.[3] More generous was the response of Sara Bloomfield, the director of the U.S. Holocaust Memorial Museum. Truman's comments were, she said, "typical of a sort of cultural anti-Semitism that was common at that time in all parts of American society. This was an acceptable way to talk."[4]

In contrast to the diary entry, in 1976 Clark Clifford, special counsel to President Truman, wrote,

> During 1947 and 1948 I heard President Truman express himself many times with reference to the Jewish problem. He had a deep, natural resentment against intolerance of any kind. He deplored the existence of Jewish ghettos and the cruel and persistent persecution. He never ceased to be horrified at the murder of some six million Jews by the Nazis. He was fully aware of the miserable status of the hundreds of thousands of Jews who had been displaced by the Second World War. As a student of the Bible, he believed in the historic justification for a Jewish homeland, and it was a conviction with him that the Balfour Declaration of 1917 constituted a solemn promise that fulfilled the age-old hope and dream of the Jewish people.[5]

Entry written on three loose pages, interleaved in the diary book and dated 6:00 P.M. Monday July 21, '47.

Had ten minutes conversation with Henry Morgenthau about Jewish ship in Palistine [sic]. Told him I would talk to Gen[eral] Marshall about it.

He'd no business, whatever to call me. The Jews have no sense of proportion nor do they have any judgement on world affairs.

Henry brought a thousand Jews to New York on a supposedly temporary basis and they stayed. When the country went backward—and Republican in the election of 1946, this incident loomed large on the D[isplaced] P[ersons] program.

The Jews, I find are very, very selfish. They care not how many Estonians, Latvians, Finns, Poles, Yugoslavs or Greeks get murdered or mistreated as DP as long as the Jews get special treatment. Yet when they have power, physical, financial or political neither Hitler nor Stalin has anything on them for cruelty or mistreatment to the under dog. Put an underdog on top and it makes no difference whether his name is Russian, Jewish, Negro, Management, Labor, Mormon, Baptist he goes haywire. I've found very, very few who remember their past condition, when prosperity comes.

Look at the Congress[ional] attitude on D[isplaced] P[ersons]—and they all come from D[isplaced] P[ersons].

Clifford's recollection, I believe, was the true Harry Truman. What worries me is that Jewish historians will ignore his lifetime of friendship with Jews and his sympathy for Jewish causes, and attempt to portray him as an anti-Semite based on a two-paragraph diary entry.

The Jewish victim mentality syndrome, which declares you cannot trust anyone, thrives on outing anti-Semites among supposed friends. I do not want to see done to Harry Truman what misguided, victim-mentality, Jewish revisionist historians have already done to Franklin D. Roosevelt.[6] I fear that they will portray his recognition of Israel as a crass political decision by a closet anti-Semite. Revisionist historians, well before the uncovering of the diary, had already begun this process. Fortunately, Michael Benson in his definitive book on the recognition of Israel discusses this revisionism and refutes it in detail.[7]

Did Truman recognize Israel simply to secure Jewish votes in the 1948 election? The evidence does not support such a claim. The Jewish vote in New York was not a factor in the recognition process. Clark Clifford reported that Truman had already written off New York due to the Henry Wallace factor (it was also the home state of his Republican opponent, Governor Thomas E. Dewey). Indeed, Truman did lose that state. If his motivation was primarily political, he would not have continued the American arms embargo against Israel throughout the election period of May to November (Israel bought its armament from Europe), and he would not have withheld de jure recognition until January of 1949, after the first elections in Israel. Truman was not pandering to the Jews. I agree with historian David McCullough, who has said that the assumption that Truman was motivated primarily by politics in his support of a Jewish state "is a cynical, unrealistic misunderstanding of the people involved."[8]

Politics aside, why was Truman so annoyed at Morgenthau and so critical of Jews in his 1947 diary entry? To put it in the vernacular, while Truman was working his tushie off to help Jews, he was the object of ever-increasing Jewish political pressure. To begin, in April of 1945 Truman assured Rabbi Stephen Wise that he didn't trust the "striped-pants boys" in the State Department.[9] In reference to them, Truman wrote in his memoirs, "I am sorry to say that there were some among them who were also inclined to be anti-Semitic."[10] Meanwhile, he was pressuring Churchill in July of 1945, and then Clement Attlee in August and November of that year, to allow another 100,000 Jews into Palestine under the British White Paper.[11] As far back as April 1943, Truman made his position clear in a speech at a Chicago Stadium rally on behalf of the doomed European Jews. Truman was not running for anything at that time and had no significant Jewish constituency in Missouri to please. Nevertheless, he proclaimed: "Today—not tomorrow—we must do all that is humanly possible to provide a haven and place of safety for all those who can be grasped from the hands of the Nazi butchers.... This is not a Jewish problem. It is an American problem—and we must and we will face it squarely and honorably."[12]

In the year immediately following World War II, the very existence of a Jewish homeland was at stake and the Jewish leadership in the United States lobbied the president with increasing intensity and as if he were an adversary to the cause. In one of his greatest understatements, Truman wrote in his memoirs, "The persistence of a few of the extreme Zionist leaders—actuated by political motives and engaging in political threats—disturbed and annoyed me."[13] In truth, he was livid.

Rabbi Abba Hillel Silver, one of the leading American Zionists of the time, actually stormed into Truman's office and pounded his fists on his desk. Abba Eban wrote, "Truman regarded Silver with severe aversion regarding him not inaccurately as a supporter of the Republican Party which came second only to the Soviet Union as a primary target of President Truman's distrust."[14] Truman wrote to David Niles, one of his advisors, in May of 1947, "We could have settled this Palestine thing if U.S. politics had been kept out of it. Terror [in Palestine] and Silver are the contributing causes of some, if not all, of our troubles."[15]

Jewish pressure for causes involving Jewish survival can become a bit heavy-handed. Concerning Israel, from 1947 to 1948 Truman received 48,600 telegrams, 790,575 postcards, and 81,200 pieces of other mail. In 1948 in one three-month period alone, he received 301,900 postcards. Benson commented, "Such a steady stream clearly annoyed the president."[16] If this issue were playing out today, I hesitate to contemplate how many e-mails he would receive.

In defense of the full-court press by the establishment Jewish leaders, it is important to understand that the measure of Truman the man that we have today was not known to them. In fact, they pressured a president who appeared to them to be wavering in his support of the new Jewish state. For example, Truman met with Chaim Weizmann on March 18, 1948, and assured him of United

States support. The very next day, without Truman's knowledge or permission, Ambassador Warren Austin at the United Nations proposed a U.N. Trusteeship over Palestine rather than a partition plan. Truman was outraged. Clark Clifford reported that Truman said to him, "'They have made me out to be a double-crosser."[17] In an interview with Jonathan Daniels, Clifford reported a slightly different reaction from Truman: "I don't understand this. How could this have happened! I assured Chaim Weizmann...he must think I'm a shitass."[18] While the president was angry and upset, Truman could not publicly acknowledge that he had lost control of his State Department. Hence, the Jewish establishment did not realize the extent of commitment that Truman had on their behalf.

Not only was Truman under pressure from the Zionist Jews, he was also pressured by both the State and Defense Departments who believed recognition of Israel would put the flow of Arab oil in danger and would open the door for an onslaught of Soviet influence among the Arab states. Clark Clifford, the presidential advisor who argued for recognition, did not attribute the State Department's opposition to anti-Semitism, but to honest policy considerations expressed by career professionals. Among those expressing opposition to the Jewish state out of national security concerns was the secretary of state. In the famous May 12, 1948, "showdown in the Oval Office," Secretary of State George Marshall stated that, if Truman were to recognize Israel he would have to vote against him in the next election, if he ever voted at all. Truman aide George Elsey put this in context: "It was essential that there not be an open break, a public break with General Marshall.... He had a reputation that was unsurpassed in our country at that time...Truman, after all, was an unelected, accidental president in the eyes of many people, and if a man like Marshall were to walk away from him, even the possibility of Truman's renomination would be in doubt."[19] Talk about pressure. Clearly, Harry Truman felt it from both sides. He wrote his sister Mary Jane, "I'm so tired and bedeviled I can't be decent to people."[20] Elsey commented, "So here was a guy under pressure, and occasionally he blew his stack.... Who wouldn't under the circumstances?"[21]

It is in this context of enormous political pressure that we should read the 1947 Diary. And add to the pressure Truman's emotional makeup. He was an emotional man and in times of great loss, prone to tears, both in public and private. When his childhood friend and press secretary Charlie Ross suddenly died of a heart attack, he broke down in tears and could not continue his press conference announcing the death.[22] David Ben-Gurion noted in his memoirs that in a New York hotel suite, when he thanked Truman for his steadfast support of Israel, tears suddenly sprang from Truman's eyes. The Jewish statesman wrote, "His eyes were still wet when he bade me good-by."[23] Abba Eban has written of an occasion in 1952 when he praised Truman in public, and recalled: "As I glanced at him he was wiping away a tear."[24]

An emotional man may also be prone to outbursts. Truman blasted the U.S. Marine Corps, accusing it of having "a propaganda machine that is almost equal to Stalin's."[25] He later made a public apology. Better he should have written his thoughts about the Marine Corps in his private diary. And, of course, the most famous demonstration of emotion came when the president excoriated the *Washington Post* music reviewer who criticized Margaret Truman's singing ability. The irate president and father was threatening to kick him in his testicles. Specifically, Truman wrote, "Some day I hope to meet you. When that happens you'll need a new nose, a lot of beefsteak for black eyes, and perhaps a supporter below!"[26]

Parenthetically, Truman was often profane and vulgar even when he was not agitated. In his memoirs he told the story of how Eddie Jacobson pleaded with him to see Chaim Weizmann. Although the president did not want a visit from another Zionist, after impassioned urgings by Jacobson, Truman agreed. What Truman left out of his memoirs was reported by Jacobson. After agreeing to meet Weizmann, Truman slowly turned around in his chair, looked at his old friend, and said, "You win, you bald-headed son-of-a-bitch...."[27]

Our task is to examine Truman's emotionalism and the pressure in historical context. Certainly, he was not politically correct by the social standards of our twenty-first century. Historian Eric Bergerud offers sound guidance when writing: "If one is going to use contemporary standards to judge the 'political correctness' of any white American born in the 19th century, I think the list receiving a passing grade would be very short."[28] Indeed, racial and religious slurs and jokes were common. At a time roughly concurrent with the Truman diary entry, I plead guilty to having enjoyed the hilarious Buddy Hackett Chinese waiter routine (one from column A and two from column B), a riff that would be considered racist and completely unacceptable today. Yet I am pretty sure that Hackett was not prejudiced against Chinese, and I am positive that I was not.

I believe that Harry Truman should be judged by his actions and writings over a lifetime of public service, not by a two-paragraph outburst. The historical record shows that he was amazingly free of prejudice, although he came from a family and region that was most prejudiced, primarily against African Americans. The record also shows that his decisions on civil rights and on Jewish issues were outstanding by any standard. I do not believe that he was a closet anti-Semite. The record shows the opposite. He was a good friend of the Jews and of Israel. And I am sure that were he alive today he would profusely apologize for his outburst, just as he did publicly to the Marines.

One last note as a Jew and a rabbi. If we analyze what Truman wrote about us, the comparison to Hitler and Stalin aside, he was not too far off the mark. He accused us of being "selfish," not caring about the Estonians, Latvians, and others. We must remember that we had just finished a war that cost over 50 million lives: we Jews were not the only ones suffering. Our Jewish strength is caring for the tribe. However, for the outside world, including our friends, it is quite possible to see this as selfishness. Truman had numerous international problems on his plate in 1947. We Jews correctly acted as if the Jewish problem were the only one around. That was our job. However, it didn't make Harry Truman's life any easier.

We must also remember that Truman included his own Baptist brethren as well as management and labor, in the groups he ranted about in his private diary. With these he included Jews, who once gaining power, will abuse it. Yes, he was ranting against the Jews in the diary, but it was not from a particular animus. He was commenting on human nature, and, unfortunately, he was probably correct.

When dissected line by line, the diary becomes less venomous. If only he had left out the Hitler and Stalin reference. But Truman was not a cold-blooded machine. What endears him to me is that as great as he was (according to the C-SPAN Historical Poll of 2000, historians rank him in a league with Washington, Lincoln, FDR, and Teddy Roosevelt), he was able to be profane and emotional. He could, and he did, mess up on more than one occasion. In other words, he was a real person. In fact, a real person who was a friend of the Jews.

Notes

[1] This excerpt is taken from the 1947 Diary (July 21 entry). Available online at www.trumanlibrary.org/diary/page21.htm.

[2] Quoted in, Richard Cohen, "In the End, Truman Got It Right," *Los Angeles Times*, July 17, 2003.

[3] *New York Times* News Service. Printed in the *Kansas City Star*, July 2003.

[4] *Washington Post*, July 11, 2003.

[5] Speech delivered before a joint session of the American Historical Society and the American Jewish Historical Society in Washington, DC, on December 28, 1976. Reprinted in *American Heritage*, April, 1977, 11.

[6] Among the revisionists is Arthur Morse (*While Six Million Died: A Chronicle of American Apathy* [New York: Random House, 1968]). The revisionist historians argue that FDR should have either bombed the death camps or the railroad lines leading to them. They generally conclude that FDR cared little about Jews, even though he was revered at the time by the Jewish community. In answer to the revisionists, I recommend a seminal article by William J. Vanden Heuvel, "America and the Holocaust" (*American Heritage* 50, no. 4 [July–August 1999]: 35–52) and a compendium of monographs by fifteen scholars in Michael Neufeld and Michael Berenbaum's *The Bombing of Auschwitz: Should the Allies Have Attempted It* (New York: St Martin's Press, 2000). In that book, Holocaust expert Deborah Lipstadt derides the revisionist campaign to fault FDR as an ex post facto writing of history by neoconservatives. The respected Jewish historian of World War II Gerhard Weinberg actually argues that the American policy of victory in the shortest time (which meant that no air power was diverted to bomb the camps) actually saved Jewish lives, for every day the war continued more Jews were led to the ovens. There was a real moral problem in bombing the camps and killing some Jews to save potential future inmates, and most experts believed that the railroad line would have been quickly repaired, thereby negating Allied objectives. George Elsey, an aide to FDR and Truman, commented in a June 2004 letter to me, "Based on the reports we saw of the surprising rapidity with which the Nazis were able to repair damage to their railroad system inflicted by Allied air raids, I agree with the statement (your quote of Gerhard Weinberg) that the more bombings would have had little effect on their murderous efforts."

[7] Michael T. Benson, *Harry S. Truman and the Founding of Israel* (Westport, CT: Praeger, 1997).

[8] Author David McCullough made this statement in an interview with Michael Benson in 1993; quoted in Benson, *Truman and the Founding of Israel*, 6. See also Michael Gardner, *Harry S. Truman and Civil Rights: Moral Courage and Political Risks* (Carbondale: Southern Illinois University Press, 2002), in which Gardner concludes that Truman's entire civil rights platform, including his desegregation of the military and the civil service, was contrary to political advantage. Gardner quotes White House aide General Donald Dawson: "When people on the staff would caution the president about this or that issue—claiming that public opinion was against some action that the president planned to take, Harry Truman would interrupt by asking his advisors to tell him what they thought was the best thing—the right thing for the country. It was just that simple—polls didn't matter; the good of the country did."

[9] Harry S. Truman, *Memoirs, vol. 1, Year of Decisions* (New York: Doubleday, 1955), 69.

[10] Truman, *Memoirs, vol. 2, Years of Trial and Hope* (New York: Doubleday, 1956), 164.

[11] Truman, *Memoirs*, 2:135, 145.

[12] Harry S. Truman, Speech delivered at Chicago Stadium, Chicago, Illinois, April 14, 1943. 8 PM. 1943. April 14, United Rally to Demand Rescue of Doomed

Jews, Chicago, IL, Press Release File, Speech Files, Papers as U.S. Senator and Vice President, Harry S. Truman Papers, Truman Library.

[13] Truman, *Memoirs,* 2:158.

[14] Larry S. Hackman, ed., *Harry S. Truman and the Recognition of Israel* (Independence, MO: Harry S. Truman Library, 1998), 16.

[15] Truman to David Niles, 13 May 1947—President's Secretary's Files—Palestine File, Truman Library.

[16] Benson, *Truman and the Founding of Israel,* 94.

[17] Clifford, "Recognizing Israel," 7.

[18] David McCullough, *Truman* (New York: Simon & Schuster, 1992), 611.

[19] Hackman, *Truman and the Recognition of Israel,* 12.

[20] McCullough, *Truman,* 599.

[21] Hackman, *Truman and the Recognition of Israel,* 10.

[22] McCullough, *Truman,* 827.

[23] Clifford, "Recognizing Israel," 11.

[24] Hackman, *Truman and the Recognition of Israel,* 19.

[25] Harry S. Truman to Congressman Gordon McDonough, August 29, 1950, in *Public Papers of the Presidents of the United States: Harry S. Truman, 1950* (Washington, DC: Government Printing Office, 1965), 618.

[26] McCullough, *Truman,* 829–30.

[27] For Truman's accounts of the historic meeting between Truman and Jacobson, see Truman, *Memoirs,* 2:160–161; and Merle Miller, *Plain Speaking: An Oral Biography of Harry S. Truman* (New York: Berkley Publishing, 1974), 217.

[28] Eric Bergerud, posting on h-diplo@h-net.msu.edu, 7/22/2003.

RECOGNIZING ISRAEL
"A Little Touch of Harry in the Night"

Michael T. Benson

There is a well-known anecdote about President Truman getting emotional when, following Truman's recognition of Israel, the chief rabbi of Israel came to pay the president a visit. When I first read that account, I made a list of questions I wanted to ask the famous Truman biographer David McCullough. I spent a morning with Mr. McCullough out at Martha's Vineyard when I was researching my book, *Harry S. Truman and the Founding of Israel*. He said President Truman was not one to show his emotion in public and he had only found two accounts where that happened. One was the rabbi's visit. The other was at a cabinet meeting when President Truman was informed of a cheating scandal at the United States Military Academy. I think the reason he got so emotional on that occasion was because his poor eyesight had kept him out of West Point, and he was so disappointed that these young men, to whom much had been entrusted, had let down their country by cheating.

A footnote must be added to the story of Chaim Weizmann coming to the Rose Garden at the White House and presenting President Truman with the gift of state. The photograph of the event shows President Truman looking towards the scrolls while standing next to a smiling Chaim Weizmann. Dr. Weizmann was a renowned chemist. During World War I, he developed an acetone that the British used in production of war materiel and he was widely respected in the international scientific community. He didn't smile all that often; when I interviewed Abba Eban back in 1992 he said that there was a story behind this picture. I said, "I don't know the story. Will you please tell me?" He said, "Well, Dr. Weizmann shows up at the

Dr. Chaim Weizmann, president of Israel, presents a Torah to Truman during a visit to the White House on May 25, 1948. (TL 59–848)

White House. He has a gift of state. He's now the new president of the new State of Israel and no one has any idea of what he's going to bring the president. So he shows up with this set of Torah scrolls wrapped in beautiful purple velvet with some bells hanging down from them. No one has any idea what they are. Dr. Weizmann is not well. His health is not good at all, and he's having a hard time carrying these Torah scrolls, which are actually quite heavy. Then he hands them to President Truman. I have to add parenthetically that no matter how many times Sam Rosenman told President Truman that Dr. Weizmann's given name was pronounced with a hard 'kha' sound, 'Chaim,' he always called him 'Cham.' So, Dr. Weizmann takes these Torah scrolls and hands them to President Truman. President Truman looks down at them and he says, 'Well, thanks, Cham. I've always wanted a set of these.' Right at that moment, the White House photographer snapped the picture and that's why you have both men grinning."

Studying the life and career of Harry Truman changed my life forever. The journey can be traced to a spring morning in 1992 when I entered the doors of the Truman Library for the first time. I hasten to add that my initial research visit was made possible by a generous grant from the Harry S. Truman Library Institute for National and International Affairs. I can state unequivocally that Harry Truman is my hero. For people of my generation, it might be tough to find many who list politicians among their heroes. As Truman was inclined to say, "A statesman is nothing more than a politician who has been dead for several years." But those of us who grew up in America and witnessed its presidency transformed by Watergate and subsequent scandals harken back to an era when politicians were different. There is an element to Truman that is extremely rare in today's politics. Perhaps it is best summarized by a statement made by Eric Sevareid of CBS News. He said, "I'm not sure Truman was right about the atomic bomb or even Korea. But remembering him reminds people what a man in an office ought to be like. It's character, just character. He stands like a rock in memory now."[1] Indeed, Harry Truman does stand like a rock in our nation's collective memory, as we consider many of the decisions that, when made at a time of great international tension, were incredibly difficult and complex.

Many revisionist historians in the 1960s rushed to note our thirty-third president's faults and the inherent shortcomings of his policies. Their criticisms notwithstanding, year after year the courage of Truman's actions and decisions propels him into the ranks of near-great or great presidents as determined in numerous polls of America's renowned political scientists and historians. Not bad for a man who left Washington with a 23 percent approval rating during his final year in office. That is a lower rating than Richard Nixon had when he made his famous wave from the south lawn of the White House and boarded Marine One for the last time.

I serve as the president of Snow College in central Utah, a small college in a little town called Ephraim. We have a Jewish studies program, helped along by my good friend Rabbi Shmuley Boteach. When Rabbi Boteach first visited our campus, nearly four years ago, he maintained that such a program was a natural fit in a town called Ephraim, which is located right next to Mount Nebo and just north of a city named Moab, which is on the way to Zion National Park. Clearly our Mormon settlers had a flair for the dramatic and named some of the towns of our state with beautiful names. Ever since I launched into my administrative career ten years ago at the University of Utah, I have taught a class in international relations or American history and government or the U.S. presidency each semester. I intend to do so for the rest of my academic career. Each course begins with some admonition, regardless of the year, or the course material, or the level of the students. I tell my class that President Truman often stated, "There is nothing new in the world, except the history you do not know."

In my book, I try to tell a side of Truman's recognition of the State of Israel that I believed was misrepresented and misunderstood for many years. Contrary to the view many have held and propagated for decades after his historic recognition, I contend that Truman's courageous action was not motivated by Jewish money or by the desire to win Jewish votes in the 1948 election. This was antithetical to Truman—it was simply not in his makeup. Rather, his decision was based upon, in his words, "righting an historic wrong" and fulfilling a promise made by every administration since Woodrow Wilson, and America's support for the Balfour Declaration advocating the establishment of the Jewish state in Palestine. Truman's action was founded on a fundamental commitment to do what was right, for the right reason, and at the right time. How else do we explain why Truman was willing to go up against a pantheon of political power—George C. Marshall, Robert Lovett, Dean Rusk, Dean Acheson, George F. Kennan, and James Forrestal—to name just a few? To a man, each and every one of these people opposed Truman's recognition of Israel based on geopolitical and strategic grounds. This was not passive opposition. In the case of General George Marshall, whom the president admired the most, Truman faced a severe political crisis when Marshall threatened to publicly break with the president over his stance just two days prior to the British withdrawal in May of 1948.

When asked what was most impressive about President Truman, after spending ten years of his life researching and writing about him, David McCullough responded, "Three decisions made during his presidency revealed the inner core and character of the president. The first, the Berlin airlift. He had no idea how America would pull it off, but they did it. The second was the desegregation of the armed forces—incredibly unpopular for a man from a border state whose grandparents had been slaveholders and Confederates. The final decision was the recognition of the State of Israel."[2]

Other symposiums have been held on various topics and issues related to the presidency; however, Truman's recognition of Israel stands alone in terms of sheer drama, given the mood of the American people in the mid- to late- 1940s. As a moment in history, it has it all: the forceful personality, the potential of global conflict, the emotion of post–World War II revelations concerning the Holocaust, international intrigue, political machinations, secret meetings with private promises, and of course, personal vindication and national realization.

An overlay to this entire episode is what the famed writer Barbara Tuchman would call "the spongier ground of history"—intangibles that many historians might dismiss, but are nonetheless highly relevant to a complete understanding of why Truman did what he did. These things include the friendship between the president and Eddie Jacobson, the pledge made privately by the president to the famed chemist Chaim Weizmann, the efforts of Clark Clifford to persuade Robert Lovett to persuade his boss, the secretary of state, and finally, George Marshall's decision for reasons of professional loyalty not to break publicly with the president. This is high drama indeed. Two individuals very close to this issue saw the drama in the early months of 1948. David Niles and United Nations Secretary General Trygve Lie viewed the indispensable role of Harry Truman as absolutely incontrovertible. Niles and Samuel I. Rosenman were the only Jewish White House staff members significantly involved in both the Truman and Roosevelt administrations, and on many occasions Niles expressed doubt that Israel would have come into existence if FDR had lived. I believe this to be the case, given FDR's inclination to make multiple promises to various groups. One thing is quite certain, however. One would be hard-pressed to find another president as willing as Truman was to stand up to the entire State Department and the foreign-policy–making apparatus over an issue such as Palestine. UN Secretary General Lie said, "I think we can safely say that if there had been no Harry S. Truman, there would be no Israel today."[3]

Truman's recognition of Israel, issued a mere eleven minutes after David Ben-Gurion's historic announcement in Tel Aviv almost sixty years ago, has had enormous implications for our nation's foreign policy. I still maintain that, being the student of history that he was, President Truman believed somehow, someday, peace between Arabs and Jews could be realized. He often reminded visitors of his support for both sides. Truman frequently expressed his belief that they were cousins, all descendants from Father Abraham, and they should try and live together peaceably. He believed (naively, many contend) that economics would bring the two sides together and that a Tennessee Valley Authority–type project in the Middle East would force the two sides into a codependent arrangement resulting in long-term peace. This, tragically, has never happened.

What has finally happened, however, is recognition by many that a two-state situation is the only viable and workable solution in the region. Truman and the United States embraced this in 1947 in support of the UN partition plan, even though the particulars of the plan were highly controversial and some parts were probably unworkable. The principle, nonetheless, remains the same. Truman

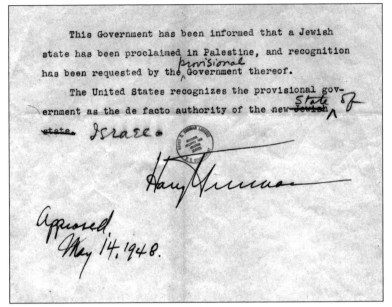

Draft press release signed by Truman, announcing U.S. recognition of the State of Israel, May 14, 1948. (Handwriting of the President, Alphabetical Correspondence File, Charles G. Rosi Papers, Truman Library)

supported a free and democratic Israel and advocated similar autonomy for the Palestinians as well. I believe Truman's place in history, as it relates to his role in recognizing the State of Israel, is best summarized by Sir Winston Churchill, "To every man, there comes that special moment, when he is figuratively tapped on the shoulder and offered a chance to do a special thing, unique to him and fitted to his talent. What a tragedy if that moment finds him unprepared or unqualified for the work which would be his finest hour." In May 1948, the moment of history and fate found Harry Truman both prepared and qualified for one of his finest hours.

Looking at their background and academic training, one would be hard-pressed to find two more polar opposites than Dean Acheson and Harry S. Truman. President Truman was the only president in the last century not to have graduated from college. Dean Acheson went to Groton; he attended Yale and Harvard Law School. He served two terms as a clerk for the United States Supreme Court, and won a Pulitzer Prize for his memoirs, *Present at the Creation*. The title page of that book reads, "to Harry Truman. The captain with the mighty heart." Acheson had enormous respect for President Truman. He recognized in him some of those intangibles that we see in great leaders. Well-versed in literature, particularly Shakespeare, Acheson would often quote a little couplet from *Henry V*. On the eve of the battle of Agincourt the British were outnumbered four to one by the French, and Shakespeare follows King Harry as he went among his troops to lift them up. This is what Shakespeare says about the impact King Harry had on his troops, and these are the lines Acheson would often quote relative to President Truman: "...every wretch, pining and pale before, / Beholding him, plucks comfort from his looks... / His liberal eye doth give to every one... / a little touch of Harry in the night."

Note

[1] Quoted in David McCullough, *Truman* (New York: Simon and Schuster, 1992), 992.

[2] David McCullough, taped interview with the author, Martha's Vineyard, MA, May 27, 1993.

[3] Quoted in Michael T. Benson, *Harry S. Truman and the Founding of Israel* (Westport, CT: Praeger, 1997), 188.

PRAGMATIC IDEALISM
Truman's Broader Middle East Policy

Tom Lansford

Harry S. Truman utilized a blend of pragmatism and idealism in both his domestic and his foreign policies. He sought lofty goals but was always aware of the limitations imposed by domestic actors and the changing circumstances of the world stage. Consequently, Truman's policy objectives were generally based on U.S. national interests. He also avoided overreach, that tendency of leaders to fail as they attempt too much. Instead, his administration pursued foreign and security objectives in the Middle East that were obtainable at a cost the American public, and Congress, would accept. Truman's recognition of Israel was demonstrative of his global idealism, while his broader Middle East policy reflected the president's political realism.

While the other sections of this book focus on Truman's recognition of Israel, this chapter concentrates on the president's overall Middle East policy. This is undertaken through an examination of the nexus of foreign and domestic policy within the United States. Robert Putnam summarized the interplay of foreign policy and domestic actors as a "two-level" game in which world leaders endeavor to meet the needs and goals of domestic groups while simultaneously achieving international victories that enhance the power and influence of their countries.[1] Hence, U.S. presidents play one game at the international level and another at the domestic level.[2] Failure to secure victories at both levels can cause gains in one category to be forfeited, as was the case with Woodrow Wilson's efforts with the League of Nations. Truman proved adept at both games and was able to develop the bipartisan consensus that not only undergirded his own initiatives in the Middle East, but laid the foundation for future national security cooperation during the Cold War.

THE BIPARTISAN CONSENSUS

From his service in the Senate, Truman understood the necessity for bipartisanship in foreign and defense policy. The president and leading Senate Republican Arthur H. Vandenberg developed a close working and personal relationship that was especially important during the period when Republicans controlled Congress (and the era of some of Truman's boldest foreign policy initiatives, including the Truman Doctrine and the Marshall Plan). Truman frequently suggested that his staff maintain contacts with leaders in both parties and he employed people on the White House staff regardless of party affiliation. Former Truman aide Ken Hechler wrote that "there never appeared to be any party loyalty test for White House staff members. Nobody seemed disturbed that I was a registered Republican when I went onto the White House payroll."[3]

Bipartisanship was both a means to accomplish goals and a goal in and of itself for the Truman administration. In 1949, the State Department issued a bulletin that declared the objective of the administration was "to achieve agreement on sound and publicly supported policy" and to "make it virtually impossible for 'momentous divisions' to occur in our foreign affairs."[4] Bipartisanship meant that Truman had to contain the leftist members of his own party to ensure the development of centrist policies. The president would be criticized by members of the liberal wing of the Democratic Party who asserted that the administration attempted to use the spirit of bipartisanship as a means to gag debate within the party and eliminate alternative strategies to confrontation with the Soviet Union.[5] Bipartisanship did not mean an end to legitimate policy differences, but rather it was the recognition that the goals and objectives of foreign and security policy were more important than minor political advantages. Truman wrote that "there were occasions when Senator Vandenberg disagreed with my policies but he never attempted to sabotage them."[6] Vandenberg wrote that bipartisanship "means that we strive by consultation to lift foreign policy above partisan issue. It means that we attempt to hammer out the greatest possible means of agreement so we can speak to the world, not as 'Republicans' or 'Democrats' but as undivided Americans."[7] It was not, however, a negotiation among equals. Truman was careful to maintain the supremacy of the presidency in foreign policy. In his memoirs, Truman observed that "bipartisanship in foreign policy means simply that the President can repose confidence in the members of the other party and that in turn the leaders of that party have confidence in the president's conduct of foreign affairs."[8]

In practice, bipartisan foreign policy formulation meant frequent private meetings and consultations between Truman, his senior staff, and leading Republicans, as well as the appointment of Republicans to posts in the State Department. In 1951, Hechler wrote a synopsis of Truman's bipartisan foreign policy that was published as a Senate report. In the document, Hechler outlined six main areas in which bipartisanship was demonstrated:

1. Frequent White House conferences with congressional leaders of both parties....
2. Bipartisan congressional representation on U.S. delegations to many international conferences.
3. The inclusion of leading members of both political parties on United States delegations to the United Nations.
4. Frequent consultation on major policies between the Department of State, and the bipartisan membership of various congressional committees....
5. The bipartisan planning and development of major policies with the assistance of congressional leaders of both parties, as well as private individuals and outside groups representing both political parties....
6. The appointment of leading members of the Republican Party to high policy positions in the Department of State, and in other agencies dealing with foreign policy matters....[9]

Truman endorsed Hechler's report and encouraged the 1952 presidential candidates to read the document.[10]

Points 5 and 6 from Hechler's report underscore the importance Truman attached to ensuring public support for his initiatives. By binding Republicans to administration policies, either because they helped craft the initiatives or because they helped implement them, Truman was able to forestall partisan criticism and bolster support for specific programs such as the Truman Doctrine, the Marshall Plan, and the creation of the North Atlantic Treaty Organization. In addition, by involving private citizens, he was able to expand the lobbying power of the White House. It also prevented embarrassing congressional defeats along the lines of the failed League of Nations. Bipartisanship assured the president of domestic wins in his two-level games. He could negotiate with, or confront, foreign leaders with the additional confidence guaranteed by the domestic support his policies enjoyed.

The advent of the Korean War and the rise of McCarthyism undermined bipartisanship. The bipartisanship of Truman and Vandenberg came under attack by the isolationist wing of the Republican Party, led by Senator Robert Taft, and the right wing of the party led by Joseph McCarthy. Taft charged that bipartisanship had become a guise for Truman to accomplish his goals with little policy debate, while McCarthy argued that the administration was "soft on communism" and that moderate Republicans were betraying the country by cooperating with the president. Nonetheless, congressional records show that in two-thirds of the votes, Taft and McCarthy and their allies voted the same as Vandenberg.[11] In spite of the rhetoric, the core principles of bipartisanship in foreign policy remained throughout the Truman presidency.

THE BEGINNINGS OF THE COLD WAR AND THE MIDDLE EAST

Truman understood that the emerging Cold War represented, at its core, a competition between democracy and free enterprise, and totalitarianism. While most Americans looked forward to a new era of peace and prosperity, the president understood that the United States faced a new struggle. Looking back at the immediate post-World War II period, Truman noted in his memoirs that the "surrender of the Axis powers did not bring any relaxation or rest for our people."[12] The 1946 report "American Relations with the Soviet Union" (commonly known as the "Clifford-Elsey Report," after its authors, Clark Clifford and George Elsey) noted that the Soviet Union was actively "seeking wherever possible to weaken the military position and influence of the United States abroad...."[13]

During World War II, British and Soviet troops invaded northern Iran in response to the pro-Axis policies of Tehran. Foreshadowing the postwar divisions in Europe, Iran was divided into three zones in 1941, a Soviet zone in the north, an autonomous Iranian area in the center, and a British zone in the south. A small number of American troops were deployed in the British zone in 1942. In the waning months of the war, Iranian officials appealed to Washington for aid in expelling the Soviets.[14] In December 1945, Moscow supported the self-proclaimed independence of two separatist provinces in the north, the Kurdish People's Republic and the autonomous

Republic of Azerbaijan. Both areas were Soviet client states. Allied troops were supposed to withdraw from Iran within six months after the end of World War II. With support from the British and Americans, Iranian government forces attacked the two breakaway republics in what was described by Iranian scholar Hassan Arfa as the first real combat of the Cold War.[15]

With support from the Truman administration, Iran appealed to the United Nations for aid in forcing a Soviet withdrawal. In January 1946, the UN Security Council adopted Resolution 2, which called on the Soviet Union and Iran to negotiate a withdrawal of Soviet forces to be complete by March 2. This was followed by two other resolutions urging Soviet withdrawal.[16] In addition, Truman demanded that Moscow withdraw its forces or face action from the United States. In an interview, Truman recalled that he instructed Secretary of State James F. Byrnes to "send a message to Stalin: 'if he doesn't get out we'll move in.'"[17] Truman's message to Stalin is the subject of debate with some scholars questioning the demarche. For instance, James A. Thorpe suggests that "the ultimatum is a myth created by Truman and perpetuated by scholars" to enhance the president's anticommunist credentials.[18] However, accounts by contemporaries support Truman's version. To demonstrate his seriousness during the crisis, Truman dispatched American naval forces to the region, and when Stalin did not withdraw by the March deadline, Truman later stated that "I sent him word I would move the fleet as far as the Persian Gulf."[19] The robust American support and international pressure resulted in a Soviet-Iranian oil agreement signed on April 4, 1946. The Soviets withdrew in May 1946. The incident had a lasting impression on Truman about the long-term intentions of Joseph Stalin toward neighboring states and the trustworthiness of the Soviet leader.[20] Truman's support for Iran during the crisis helped cement the alliance that would remain through most of the Cold War.

For Truman, the Soviet withdrawal was necessary for both idealistic and practical reasons. First, Truman was generally opposed to Soviet expansion because of his personal belief in democracy and self-rule. Second, the president believed that Soviet control of Iranian oil would undermine the global economic order and seriously erode Western Europe's ability to rebuild its shattered economies. Truman also perceived that Soviet adventurism in Iran was part of a broader strategy to gain regional ascendancy and was directly related to Stalin's attempts to gain special privileges and concessions in Turkey. If

Kurdistan and Azerbaijan remained under Soviet control, pressure on Istanbul would be increased. Consequently, Truman became determined to aid Turkey.

TURKEY, THE TRUMAN DOCTRINE, AND CONTAINMENT

In the midst of the Iranian crisis, Truman wrote to Byrnes that "there isn't a doubt in my mind that Russia intends an invasion of Turkey and seizure of the Black Sea Straits to the Mediterranean."[21] The president initiated steps to demonstrate support for Turkey, including ordering a U.S. naval force to Istanbul and increasing security negotiations with the Turkish government. The need for American action was underscored in early 1947 when the British announced that they could no longer provide military and financial support for the Greek and Turkish governments. Both states faced ongoing internal communist insurgencies and pressure from the Soviet Union. Meanwhile, Truman faced increasing tensions in Europe. The withdrawal of British troops from Greece and India was perceived by the administration as creating a dangerous power vacuum in the region that could only be ameliorated by the United States.[22] As historian David R. Devereux noted, the United States was becoming "the unwilling heir to the British mantle of power in the Middle East."[23] Truman realized that the American public was loath to engage in another global struggle of the scale of World War II; therefore, he sought to craft a policy that would prevent Soviet expansion without a wartime military and economic mobilization.

Containment was the answer. The administration developed the containment policy based on the recommendations of the Clifford-Elsey Report and the writings of George Kennan, a diplomat at the State Department, whose famous Long Telegram was reprinted in the influential journal *Foreign Affairs*. Kennan asserted that if the United States prevented Soviet expansion, it would cause the Soviet Union to eventually collapse. He wrote that "the issue of Soviet-American relations is in essence a test of the overall worth of the United States as a nation among nations. To avoid destruction the United States need only measure up to its own best traditions and prove itself worthy of preservation as a great nation."[24]

Containment was, in many ways, an ideal strategy for the Truman administration, for it allowed the president to avoid large-scale military conflicts and to balance defense spending with domestic

*President Truman addressing a joint session of Congress, March 12, 1947. His
"Truman Doctrine" speech asked Congress to appropriate $400,000 in financial
and military aid to Greece and Turkey to bolster the Middle East against the spread
of Soviet totalitarianism. (Photo collection, Truman Library)*

programs. Containment was embodied in the 1947 Truman Doctrine, which pledged American support for countries facing communist insurgencies, initially $400 million for Greece and Turkey. In
the Doctrine, Truman declared: "Should we fail to aid Greece and
Turkey in this fateful hour, the effect will be far-reaching to the
West as well as to the East."[25] The president also made it clear that
the United States would be succeeding the British and would emerge
as the main deterrent to Soviet aggression in the area. Truman stated
that "the British government, which has been helping Greece, can
give no further financial or economic aid after March 1 [1947]" and
that Britain could "no longer extend financial or economic aid to
Turkey."[26] The president further noted that "Great Britain finds
itself under the necessity of reducing or liquidating its commitments
in several parts of the world, including Greece."[27] However, mindful
of the need for domestic support, Truman's staff conducted a series

of reports on public reaction to his request for aid and his decision to undertake measures without involving the United Nations. One report noted that among newspaper editorials, "a sizable group is 100 percent in favor of the president's proposal" and "on the president proposing action outside of the United Nations, opinion is four to one in favor of such action."[28]

CONTAINMENT IN THE GREATER MIDDLE EAST

The Truman Doctrine had unintended consequences. The willingness of the United States to successfully challenge the Soviet Union over Iran and to provide military and economic aid to Turkey led countries in the region to seek closer ties with the United States. For instance, Shah Mahmud, the leader of Afghanistan, noted in 1946 that he was

> convinced that America's championship of the small nations guarantees my country's security against aggression. America's attitude is our salvation. For the first time in our history we are free of the threat of great powers using our mountain passes as pathways to empire. Now we can concentrate our talents and resources on bettering the living conditions of our people.[29]

The United States was also perceived as a neutral party that did not have the same imperialist tendencies as Britain, France, or Russia.

The Truman administration was careful with its aid dollars as policy makers meticulously calculated the costs and benefits of new alliances and the willingness of the American public to devote resources to foreign countries. For example, an Afghan delegation visited Washington with a request for economic development aid. They were turned down by the State Department, which noted the request lacked specificity.[30] The following year, the Afghans returned with a request and attempted, as other states would, to secure U.S. assistance by threatening to turn to the Soviet Union if they were rebuffed. In its summary of the request, the State Department noted that the Afghans argued their request was "of political as well as economic importance; possibly increasingly so in light of manifestations of Soviet interest and offers to be of assistance to Afghanistan."[31] The Afghans were granted a loan worth $21 million to develop water resources in the south of the country.[32] They were denied military aid, however. The Defense Department asserted that "Afghanistan is of little or no strategic importance to the United States.... Its geographic location coupled with the realization by

Afghan leaders of Soviet capabilities presages Soviet control of the country whenever the international situation so dictates."[33]

The calculated neglect of states such as Afghanistan was in contrast to U.S. policy toward states it deemed strategically important such as Iran, Turkey, and Saudi Arabia. While the Truman administration generally accepted that the kingdoms of the Persian Gulf were part of the British sphere of influence, Washington increasingly strengthened its ties with Saudi Arabia in the late 1940s and early 1950s because of the kingdom's strategic and economic importance. At the end of World War II, the United States received permission to build an air base at Dhahran, Saudi Arabia. After the war, America continued to lease the base from the Saudi government and even expand it. For the Saudis, the U.S. military presence provided reassurance at a time of perceived weakening of the British commitment to the region, even though the presence of American troops created controversies within the Saudi religious community (a trend that would continue). Staunch British support, including military support and training, for the traditional rivals of the Saudis—the Hashemites of Jordan and Iraq—led the Saudis to agree to a long-term lease of the Dhahran airfield. In addition, in 1951, the Truman administration signed a mutual defense agreement with Saudi Arabia.

ISRAEL AND THE ARABS

Fighting between the British, Jews, and Arabs, combined with Truman's deep feelings about the Holocaust, led to American support for the creation of a Jewish state in the British colony of Palestine. Truman endorsed the British request for a UN recommendation to resolve the fighting in 1947 and initially supported the subsequent plan to create two states: Israel and Palestine. Israel would receive 57 percent of the land, and the Arabs 43 percent along with UN administration of Jerusalem. Truman understood the potential for further conflict and noted that he was "fully aware of the Arabs' hostility to Jewish settlement in Palestine."[34] Nonetheless, at first he believed the solution was the most pragmatic method to deal with the ongoing conflict and to prevent regional instability. In addition, domestic support for the establishment of a Jewish state weighed heavily in Truman's calculations. The president later wrote,

> The White House, too, was subjected to a constant barrage. I do not think I ever had as much pressure and propaganda aimed at the White House as I had in this instance. The persistence of a few

of the extreme Zionist leaders—actuated by political motives and engaging in political threats—disturbed and annoyed me.[35]

Israel emerged as the most significant two-level game in Truman's Middle East policy. The president had to balance domestic considerations with the need to maintain the emerging anti-Soviet coalition, especially among Muslim states such as Iran, Turkey, and Saudi Arabia. The Truman administration engaged a range of diplomatic efforts to gain regional and international support for a Jewish state and to ensure that the UN plan was adopted. Undersecretary of State Sumner Welles summarized the effort:

> By direct order of the White House every form of pressure, direct and indirect, was brought to bear by American officials upon those countries outside of the Moslem world that were known to be either uncertain or opposed to partition. Representatives or intermediaries were employed by the White House to make sure that the necessary majority would at length be secured.[36]

Truman's efforts succeeded when the General Assembly voted in favor of the two-state solution by a vote of thirty-three in favor and thirteen opposed. On May 14, 1948, the British withdrew and Truman offered diplomatic recognition to Israel.

Truman's decision to establish diplomatic relations with the new state was partially the result of idealism—his belief in the justness of a Jewish state. He even defied his closest advisors, including Secretary of State George Marshall, who opposed recognition. Under pressure from Marshall and officials at the State Department, the president did agree to postpone recognition until after Israel was formed. Undersecretary of State Robert A. Lovett proclaimed that "the President's advisors, having failed…to make the President a father of the new state have determined at least to make him the midwife."[37] The decision was also the result of domestic political considerations, especially in light of the upcoming 1948 elections and the importance of the Jewish voters in New York with its 47 electoral votes.[38] Some historians have suggested that recognition was mainly the result of electoral calculations, especially in light of the victory of pro-Zionist candidate Leo Isacson in a special election in New York in February 1948.

Truman also foresaw that Israel would by necessity be a close ally to the United States in a region still dominated by British and French colonial powers. However, he sought to minimize the estrangement with the Arab states. He agreed to an arms embargo advocated by State Department officials such as Loy Henderson, chief of Near Eastern and African affairs. Henderson and supporters of the arms embargo convinced Truman that it was one thing to recognize Israel, but the possibility of U.S. arms being used against Arabs could escalate tensions with Washington to an unacceptable level. He also pointed out that without an embargo, American weapons could be sold to Arabs and used against Israelis. Henderson asserted that an arms embargo was necessary "so long as the tension continues. Otherwise, the Arabs might use arms of U.S. origin against Jews, or Jews might use them against Arabs. In either case, we would be subject to bitter recrimination."[39] The embargo was not ended until August 4, 1949, when Israel finalized armistice agreements with the neighboring Arab states and those involved in the war for independence.

CONCLUSION

The administration's parsimony in foreign and military aid loosened with the start of the Korean War. By 1950, the United States was already providing $1 billion per year to Western Europe in military aid, including 134,000 tons of arms and equipment.[40] That figure would rise as would overall American aid. Truman had hoped to use economic and technical assistance to counter Soviet expansion. His 1949 Point Four program, announced in his inaugural address, asserted that U.S. foreign policy would be based on (1) the United Nations, (2) the ongoing economic recovery program in Europe, (3) support for nations confronting communist insurgencies or other attempts to undermine governments, and (4) a new program to disseminate U.S. technical and expert advice to promote economic development, food production, and health care. Countries such as Iran and Turkey received Point Four funding and American training for their citizens. However, Truman understood that the Korean War changed the international arena. He noted that "the attack upon Korea makes it plain beyond all doubt that communism has passed beyond the use of subversion to conquer independent nations and will now use armed invasion and war."[41]

Stalemated in Korea, Truman increased foreign and security assistance. He also sought to rebuff domestic criticisms that his administration was losing the Cold War. The United States became more proactive in dispersing international aid and more willing to develop close ties with anticommunist regimes. Military aid was increased to countries in the Middle East, including Iran and Iraq. The Truman administration also committed to significant military aid to Pakistan, following increasing Indian neutrality and successive diplomatic initiatives by Karachi. Nevertheless, the focus of the administration remained on Korea and Europe. Truman's final years in office witnessed new initiatives, including the European Defense Community, designed to enhance transatlantic security in the face of a potential Soviet invasion and to mollify domestic critics. Truman found new challenges in both the domestic and international settings and increasing spillover from both.

The ability of Truman to gain both domestic and international victories laid the foundation for the Cold War consensus on foreign policy. The president's Middle East policy reflected the interplay of idealism and realism, combined with the need to satisfy domestic audiences and to realize global goals. His policies reflected the effort to match commitments with capabilities and to maintain bipartisanship. In the Middle East, countries facing the most significant threats from Soviet expansion or regional instability received the greatest aid and support from the United States. Israel was the major exception to Truman's realism, yet U.S. recognition was a manifestation of Truman's idealism, combined with the expression of American public preferences for the region.

Notes

[1] Robert Putnam, "Diplomacy and Domestic Politics: The Logic of Two-Level Games," *International Organization* 42, no. 3 (Summer 1988): 434.

[2] Robert Putnam, "Two-Level Games: The Impact of Domestic Politics on Transatlantic Bargaining," in America and Europe in an Era of Change, ed. Helga Haftendorn and Christian Tuschoff (Boulder, CO: Westview Press, 1993), 77.

[3] Ken Hechler, *Working with Truman: Personal Memoir of the White House Years* (1982; repr., Columbia: University of Missouri Press, 1996), 25.

[4] Ernest Gross, "What Is a Bipartisan Foreign Policy?" *Department of State Bulletin* 21 (October 3, 1949): 504–5.

[5] Henry W. Berger, "Bipartisanship, Senator Taft and the Truman Administration," *Political Science Quarterly* 90, no. 2 (Summer 1975): 226.

[6] Harry S. Truman, *Memoirs,* vol. 2, *Years of Trial and Hope, 1946–1952* (1956; repr., New York: Signet, 1965), 487–88.

[7] Arthur H. Vandenberg Jr., ed. *The Private Papers of Senator Vandenberg* (Boston: Houghton Mifflin, 1952), 451.

[8] Truman, *Memoirs,* 2:488.

[9] U.S. Congress, *Review of Bipartisan Foreign Policy Consultations since World War II,* 82nd Cong., 1st sess. Senate doc. no. 87 (October 20, 1951), quoted in Hechler, *Working with Truman,* 158.

[10] U.S. Congress, *Review of Bipartisan Foreign Policy Consultations,* quoted in Hechler, *Working with Truman,* 158.

[11] Berger, "Bipartisanship," 229.

[12] Truman, *Memoirs,* 2:134.

[13] Clark Clifford and George Elsey, "American Relations with the Soviet Union" (September 24, 1946), 4; Rose Conway Files, Truman Papers, Truman Library.

[14] Stephen L. McFarland, "A Peripheral View of the Origins of the Cold War: The Crises in Iran, 1941–47," *Diplomatic History* 4 (Fall 1980), reprinted as "The Iranian Crisis of 1946 and the Onset of the Cold War," in *Origins of the Cold War: An International History,* ed. Melvyn P. Leffler and David S. Painter (London: Routledge, 1994), 242, 247.

[15] Hassan Arfa, *Under Five Shahs* (New York: William Morrow, 1965), 346.

[16] With the Soviet representative absent, the Security Council declared in Resolution 5 on May 8, 1946, that it would consider "further proceedings" against Moscow if Tehran did not report that all Soviet troops had been withdrawn; United Nations Security Council Resolution 5 (May 8, 1946).

[17] Harry S. Truman, "Interview Summary: Foreign Policy Notes on Marshall Plan, Iran and Western Union," Memoir Files, Post-Presidential Papers, Harry S. Truman Papers, Truman Library.

[18] James A. Thorpe, "Truman's Ultimatum to Stalin on the Azerbaijan Crisis: The Making of a Myth," *The Journal of Politics* 40, no. 1 (February 1978): 188.

[19] Harry S. Truman, *Truman Speaks* (New York: Columbia University Press, 1960), 71.

[20] J. Philipp Rosenberg, "The Cheshire Ultimatum: Truman's Message to Stalin in the 1946 Azerbaijan Crisis," *The Journal of Politics* 41, no. 3 (August 1979): 937.

[21] Harry S. Truman, *Memoirs,* vol.1, *Year of Decisions* (1955; repr., New York: Signet, 1965), 551–52. Harry S. Truman, *Memoirs,* vol. 1, *Year of Decisions* (1955; repr., New York: Signet, 1965), 551–52.

[22] Tom Lansford, *The Lords of Foggy Bottom: The American Secretaries of State and the World They Shaped* (New York: George Kurian Reference Books, 2001), 356–57.

[23] David R. Devereux, *The Formulation of British Defense Policy toward the Middle East, 1948–56* (London: Macmillan, 1990), 2.

[24] George Kennan, "The Sources of Soviet Conduct," *Foreign Affairs* (1947), reprinted in *Foreign Affairs* 65 (1987): 868.

[25] Harry S. Truman, "Special Message to the Congress on Greece and Turkey: The Truman Doctrine," March 12, 1947, in *Public Papers of the Presidents, Harry S. Truman, 1947* (Washington, DC: U.S. Government Printing Office, 1963), 176–80.

[26] Ibid.

[27] Ibid.

[28] Division of Press Intelligence, Office of Government Reports, "Editorial Reaction to Current Issues: The President's Address Before Congress on the Greek Situation," Part I (March 19, 1947), 1 (online at http://www.trumanlibrary.org/whistlestop/study_collections/doctrine/large/documents/index.php?documentdate=1947-03-19&documentid=4&studycollectionid =TDoctrine&pagenumber=1).

[29] *New York Times* (August 9, 1946), quoted in J. C. Hurewitz, *Middle East Politics: The Military Dimension* (New York: Praeger, 1969), 300–301.

[30] U.S. Department of State, *Foreign Relations of the United States, 1948,* vol. 5, no. 1, *The Near East, South Asia, and Africa* (Washington, DC: U.S. Government Printing Office, 1975), 488–90.

[31] U.S. Department of State, *Foreign Relations of the United States, 1948,* vol. 5, no. 1, *The Near East, South Asia, and Africa,* 490.

[32] U.S. Department of State, *Foreign Relations of the United States, 1949,* vol. 6, no. 1, *The Near East, South Asia, and Africa* (Washington, DC: U.S. Government Printing Office, 1977), 1779.

[33] U.S. Department of Defense, The Declassified Documents 1979 Collection (Washington, DC: U.S. Government Printing Office, 1979), quoted in Harry S. Bradsher, *Afghanistan and the Soviet Union* (Durham, NC: Duke University Press, 1983), 19. Instead of military aid to states such as Afghanistan, the Defense Department recommended providing $75 million to rebel groups fighting the Chinese communists in Tibet and other areas.

[34] Truman, *Memoirs,* 2:133.

[35] Ibid, 158.

[36] Sumner Welles, *We Need Not Fail* (Boston: Houghton Mifflin, 1948), 63.

[37] U.S. Department of State, *Foreign Relations of the United States, 1948*, vol. 5, no. 2, *The Near East, South Asia, and Africa* (Washington, DC: U.S. Government Printing Office, 1975), 1007.

[38] John Snetsinger, *Truman, the Jewish Vote and the Creation of Israel* (Stanford, CA: Hoover Institution Press, 1974), 78–81.

[39] Loy Henderson, quoted in *Foreign Relations of the United States, 1947*, vol. 5, no. 2, *The Near East, South Asia, and Africa.*

[40] U.S. Department of Defense, *Semiannual Report of the Secretary of Defense,* 1950 (Washington, DC: U.S. Government Printing Office, 1950), 2.

[41] Harry S. Truman, "Statement on June 27, 1950," *Department of State Bulletin* 22 (July 3, 1950): 5.

An Act of Political Courage

Asher Naim

In order to understand President Truman's decisions on the issues in the Middle East, including the recognition of Israel in 1948, one must look at the international political contest in the years immediately following World War II. The decline of the Western European powers, the expansionist policies of Marshal Joseph Stalin and the Soviets, and the assumption of a new role of leadership in international affairs by the United States are factors that must be considered.

At the end of the Second World War, the British Empire was in shambles. In succession, India, Burma, Egypt, Uganda, and Kenya all broke away in the decade or so after the war. The empire was nothing like what it had been before the war. Meanwhile, in Palestine the British faced a crisis. The Balfour Declaration of 1917 had called for a Jewish homeland in Palestine. British diplomacy brought about this declaration, and in Britain and elsewhere, it was endorsed by liberal organizations committed to establishing both an Arab and a Jewish state in Palestine. The British received a mandate after World War I to create a Jewish state in Palestine under a League of Nations resolution. In my view, the British failed to fulfill their obligation in the decades between the world wars; and in the years immediately following World War II, the British government began to back away from its commitment to the Balfour Declaration. They threw the whole issue of a Jewish homeland onto the newly created United Nations.

The United Nations was not a very self-confident organization in the mid-1940s, and therefore created a commission under UNESCO that called for a Palestinian state and a Jewish state, with Jerusalem under an international governing authority. The commission's resolution for partition passed by a two-thirds majority in the UN. I remember as a young boy in Tel Aviv counting the votes of the member nations. About this time, Palestine had a population of about 1,200,000 Arabs and 650,000 Jews. Violence erupted all over Palestine. It was so bad one could not leave home or go to a place of work. Who was right? What was justice in this complex situation?

U.S. Secretary of Defense James Forrestal was adamantly opposed to partition and wanted the entire matter reconsidered by the United Nations. He seemed to be pushing for a new plan that would not include a Jewish state in Palestine. Of course, U.S. Secretary of State George C. Marshall also opposed partition and his view affected the entire U.S. State Department. The confrontation between the State Department and the White House became obvious in the United Nations, to the point where Eleanor Roosevelt, a member of the U.S. delegation to the UN, threatened to resign her position.

Meanwhile, the majority of the United States House and Senate favored partition. They saw Israel's claim for a homeland as a legitimate aspiration. Of course, there were significant Jewish populations in states with large congressional delegations, namely New York, Pennsylvania, and Illinois, and the elected representatives from these states had to consider the Jewish votes. That is the way representative government works. Every group in a democratic society has the right to express its interests. Of course, Jewish votes were no different.

As for President Truman, he had a profound personal interest in the Middle East. His fascination was not only from his study of the Bible. Truman found the Middle East to be the most interesting and complicated area in the entire world, and he would frequently point out that there had been constant warfare in the region since ancient times. Truman felt it was a pity that political conflicts had kept the Middle East from economic development that would improve the lives of all the people in the region.

When Truman told his senior cabinet members that he planned to recognize the State of Israel on May 15, 1948, the day the last British troops were to depart from Palestine, there was concern that many U.S. State Department officials would resign. Secretary of State Marshall had expressed the strongest possible opposition to recognition, as had Secretary of Defense Forrestal. But Truman acted on his personal convictions rather than on the arguments of his closest advisors or on political expediency. He did what he thought was right; and given the pressure he was under, his decision demonstrated political courage.

THE TRUMAN DOCTRINE AND THE RECOGNITION OF ISRAEL

Pat Schroeder

When I was a little girl, I had a great-uncle who looked just like President Truman and the big buzz in our family was the possibility that we just might be fifth cousins to Harry Truman, or perhaps something like that. When you're a child and one of your favorite uncles looks like Harry Truman, strange things happen. You walk down the street and people come over and say, "Oh! Are you...?" So, I became very protective of this great-uncle. Let me tell you, life was really quite different at the time. I remember one man coming over and screaming at my uncle, "Why can't you call a shovel a shovel? Why do you insist on calling it a goddamned spade?" If you're eight years old, you're thinking, "Whoo! This is really interesting. People have some pretty strong feelings about this President Truman!"

When Harry Truman became president, the American people did not know him. At the 1944 Democratic Convention, the party leaders insisted on dropping Vice President Henry Wallace from the ticket, and Truman had emerged as their choice only as an available compromise candidate. Roosevelt accepted the political leaders' selection of Truman, but he didn't exactly put his arms around him and say, "This is my guy!" During Truman's eighty-two days as vice president, he and Roosevelt hardly ever met, and at no time was Truman allowed a public platform. Roosevelt continued to dominate the political landscape, as he had done for more than a decade. When the American people woke up one day in April 1945 and found out Harry Truman was president, they wondered, "Who is this fellow? How did he get to be president?"

In his first year in office, Truman was beset by almost unimaginable problems. In April 1945, he still had a horrendous world war on his hands and needed to end it. He had a bunch of mad liberals in his own party (and believe me, mad liberals can be a real load), and many in his initial cabinet and White House staff were Roosevelt men with no loyalty or particular liking for the new president from a small town in the Midwest with no Harvard education. In 1946, the Republicans took control of Congress and now the nervous Nellies among the Democrats were starting to ask, What's going to happen to our party in 1948? Whom can we find to run for president other than Truman? How can Truman lead us through these perilous times?

Truman was faced with numerous decisions on world affairs, the economy, racial relations, and atomic energy that would set the direction of the nation for the remainder of the twentieth century, and he faced his challenges with a steady and determined attitude. He had the wonderful ability to be himself. He never pretended to have gravitas. He did not try to play a role that was not genuine Truman. He was the real deal, and America at that time was not used to the real deal. His predecessor, FDR, had a carefully managed public image as a suave, sophisticated, solid, family man. So well-managed was his image that people did not even know that Roosevelt couldn't walk.

In 1947, Truman made a decision that would make the recognition of Israel possible one year later. That decision was to provide massive aid to the governments of Greece and Turkey, both of which were under severe pressure from the Soviet Union. In February of 1947, the British made it known that they planned to remove their military from Greece in six weeks. The British had 40,000 troops in Greece, and neighboring Bulgaria and Albania had already fallen under communist domination. So the removal of British military support for the conservative and anticommunist government of Greece presented a grim situation. Meanwhile, the Soviet Union demanded that Turkey cede part of Anataba to the Soviet State of Georgia, and give up the Dardanelles as well. The Soviet threat to expand communism to Greece and Turkey was ominous, but the governments in these countries had few friends in the United States. Turkey had remained neutral throughout most of World War II, and the elements in the Greek government favored the Nazis before Greece was invaded by the Axis powers in 1941. It was hard to make a case for saving the Greek monarchy. While Truman was advocating assistance to Greece for strategic reasons, the mayor of New

York City stated that no American boy should die to save an unpopular Greek king. The mayor noted that during World War II we had communists helping us fight Nazism and now we were willing to help Nazis fight communists. The president not only had to push his Truman Doctrine through a Congress controlled by Republicans, he had to get members of his own Democratic Party on board. From Key West, Florida, where he sought much-needed rest, the president described his thoughts on the emerging Cold War in extremely personal terms to his daughter Margaret (even taking time to offer her a bit of encouragement after a disappointing concert performance):

Key West, Florida
March 13, 1947

Dear Margie:—We had a very pleasant flight from Washington. Your old dad slept for 750 or 800 miles—three hours—and we were making from 250 to 300 miles an hour. No one not even me (your mother would say I) knew how very tired and worn to a frazzle the chief executive had become. This terrible decision I had to make had been over my head for about six weeks. Although I knew at Potsdam that there is no difference in totalitarian or police states, call them what you will, Nazi, Fascist, Communist or Argentine Republics. You know there never was but one idealistic example of communism. That is described in the Acts of the Apostles.

The attempt of Lenin, Trotsky, Stalin, et al. to fool the world and the American crackpots' association, represented by Joe Davies, Henry Wallace, Claude Pepper and the actors and artists in immoral Greenwich Village, is just like Hitler's and Mussolini's so-called socialist states.

Your pop had to tell the world just that in polite language.

Now in addition to that terrible—and it is terrible—decision, your good old 94-year-old grandmother of the 1880 generation was unlucky and broke her leg—you—the "apple of my eye"—my sweet baby always had bad luck with your first appearance. Well daughter the dice roll—sometimes they are for you—sometimes they are not. But I earnestly believe they were for you this time. I am just as sure as I can be that Sunday night at 8:00 P.M. another great soprano will go on the air. So don't worry about anything—just go on and sing as you sang that "Home Sweet Home" record for your dad—and nothing can stop you—even the handicap of being the Daughter of President Truman!

Then you come back to the White House and let me arrange a nice warm rest for you and your lovely mammy and we'll go on from there.

You must learn self-discipline—that is you must eat what you should, drink what you should—and above all sleep at night and always give people the benefit of good intentions until they are proven bad. Don't put our comfort and welfare above those around you. In other words be a good commonsense Missouri woman—daughter of your mother—in my opinion the greatest woman on earth—I want you to be second.

More love than you can realize now.

Dad

The Truman Doctrine was ultimately approved by Congress, and the aid to Greece and Turkey saved those countries from communist rule. Truman's policy solidified the eastern Mediterranean and made it possible for the nation of Israel to come into existence.

Truman dealt with so many critical international issues during his presidency that it is simply amazing. How could such an unlikely leader emerge and provide enlightened and farsighted leadership? To me, Truman appears like Queen Elizabeth I in many respects. One of my favorite books (remember I'm in the publishing business these days) is *Elizabeth I, CEO*,[1] and I find Truman and Elizabeth have a lot in common. Like Truman, Elizabeth came to power under unusual circumstances. Her claim to rule was questioned by her own sister! Her divided nation had just emerged from a series of religious wars and she was forced to address all sorts of foreign threats that must have appeared overwhelming to her contemporaries. People initially questioned the ability of the little red-headed young woman, just as they questioned the one-time haberdasher. But they were both bright, open-minded, and determined to follow courses they believed to be right; and in the end, both were recognized as great leaders.

Note

[1] Alan Axelrod, *Elizabeth I, CEO: Strategic Lessons from the Leader Who Built an Empire* (Paramus, NJ: Prentice Hall, 2000).

Remembering President Truman

Ken Hechler

I enjoy so much visiting elementary schools to talk about President Truman because the uninhibited comments that you get from second- and third-graders are so terrific. This is a little bit before peer pressure guides our conformity and political correctness. Not long ago, I was visiting a second grade and I was trying to explain to them about who Harry Truman was. I said he grew up in Independence, Missouri, and that was a very wonderful place to grow up because Truman was independent, and Independence is located in Jackson County. As a teacher, I always liked to engage the students with a little dialogue, so I said, "Which of you second-graders can tell me the great American after whom Jackson County was named?" And immediately a second grader in the back jumped up and blurted out, "Michael Jackson!"

I consider myself to be the luckiest man alive to have worked on the staff of President Harry Truman. I got to travel with him to Key West and also to go with him on trips. The president's daughter, Margaret, used to tell the president that the Truman campaign train was the only campaign train that carried its own "heckler" right on board.

Reference was made earlier to a man for whom I worked for about a quarter of a century who was a close associate of both Franklin Roosevelt and Harry Truman—Judge Samuel I. Rosenman. I asked Judge Rosenman one day, "What was the real difference between Franklin D. Roosevelt and Harry Truman?" Now, Rosenman was a member of the New York Assembly when FDR was running for governor in 1928. FDR tapped him to be his chief speechwriter. He spent seventeen years with Franklin—valuable years. Harry Truman recognized his talents and retained him; and

Sam Rosenman was the architect of two great speeches: the 21-point program in the fall of 1945 in which President Truman came out for health care for all Americans, and the acceptance speech at the 1948 Democratic National Convention. Rosenman said something very perceptive; he said the real difference between Roosevelt and Truman was that Roosevelt usually considered the political effects of what he was going to do and that Harry Truman never considered the political fallout from his decisions.

Rosenman was succeeded by Clark Clifford, who was then succeeded by a very mild-mannered, soft-spoken North Carolinian named Charles Murphy. Murphy told me one day, "Don't ever try to mention, in any proposal that you make to President Truman, what the political advantage would be, because he would immediately reject it."

I think Truman's decision on Israel can be most easily explained by the second sign that he had on his desk. Everybody knows about the most important sign: "The Buck Stops Here." But the second sign was one that very few people know about. It was a quotation from Mark Twain, and was in Mark Twain's own handwriting. It sat on President Truman's desk and he followed it very religiously. That sign said, "Always do right. This will gratify some of the people and astonish the rest." This explains, I think, the decision on Israel. It also explains other tough decisions Truman made, such as the desegregation of the armed forces and the federal government through two executive orders. He did this without wide agitation in the country for what he did. In fact, he did this in the face of public opinion that was very much against both desegregating the federal government and integrating the armed forces.

President Truman had a genuine liking for all people of different religious faiths, and both his friends and his staff included many different types of people. Everyone is familiar with his close friendship with Eddie Jacobson, which started when they ran a highly successful canteen during artillery training before World War I, followed by their partnership in Truman's haberdashery business, which eventually failed. Jacobson later played a crucial role in arranging the important meeting between Truman and the highly respected Zionist Chaim Weizmann at a time when Truman was getting increasingly upset with the unreasonable pressure of radical Zionists in this country. Judge Rosenman was not only a high-ranking White House staff member, but also a social companion. Judge Rosenman and his wife accompanied the Trumans on a European trip after Truman left the presidency. Among the Jewish White House staff members were David Niles, Assistant Press Secretary Irving Perlmeter, Special Assistants Milton Kayle and Richard Neustadt, and Personnel Officer Martin Friedman.

Truman's positive feeling toward Israel is predictable when considering the major address which he delivered on April 14, 1943, as a U.S. Senator, at the Chicago Stadium. In his address, he stated unequivocally, "Today—not tomorrow—we must do all that is humanly possible to provide a haven and place of safety for all those who can be grasped from the hands of the Nazi butchers. Free land must be opened to them."[1]

It was certainly a wonderful thing to be able to come down to Key West here with President Truman. He used his time here at the Little White House not only to recharge his batteries, but also to think and read, and to develop the vision that he had for the future. It was on such occasions that he honed his determination to do what was right with relation to Israel, the Middle East, and other parts of the world.

Note

[1] Harry S. Truman, Speech delivered at Chicago Stadium, Chicago, Illinois, April 14, 1943. 8 PM.1943. April 14, United Rally to Demand Rescue of Doomed Jews, Chicago, IL, Press Release File, Speech Files, Papers as U.S. Senator and Vice President, Harry S. Truman Papers, Truman Library.

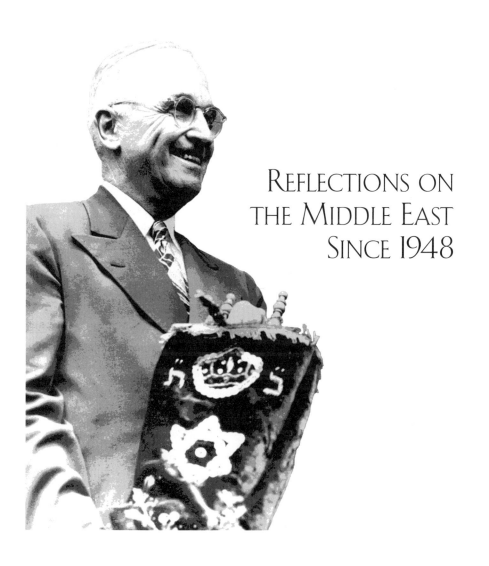

REFLECTIONS ON THE MIDDLE EAST SINCE 1948

Understanding Historical Narratives

David Gordis

In 1948, fifty-seven years ago, I was a very young man, and at that time our lives were focused on the two epochal events in the life of the Jewish community: the Holocaust and the establishment of the State of Israel. Related to these events, the incident I remember, one that is indelibly inscribed in my mind, was going to what was then known as Idlewild Airport (now evolved into John F. Kennedy International Airport). I was not flying anywhere at the time. The trip was simply to go up onto the observation roof of one of the few buildings to see the first airplane that bore the blue and white insignia of the Israeli airline. It was the only plane that El Al had, just a Bristol Britannia, a turboprop plane. However, what was dramatic about the plane was that it existed at all. In other words, the difference between having no planes and no airline and now possessing one plane is far greater—far, far more transformative—than having one plane and then having a hundred planes. That was an epochal moment. Now that single moment as a child, standing and looking at that plane with tears coming to my eyes, came after having heard not very many years earlier the reports of 1942 and 1943 about what was happening in Europe. Then came the news that the Jewish state was established. I also remember sitting by the radio and hearing the account of the United Nations vote, country by country, from Lake Success. As we listened, we wondered which country was going to put it over and approve the partition of Palestine into a Jewish state? These were moments which were, for me, unforgettable.

I want to recall another image, a photograph that has become something of a classic. It is the famous picture of President Truman with the first president of Israel, Chaim Weizmann. Weizmann was handing a gift—a Torah scroll—to Truman in gratitude and commemoration for what he had done. Here was this photograph of Weizmann, a scientist, a nonreligious Jew, handing to a Baptist, American president what was the only thing possible to represent the gratitude of the Jewish people for what had happened. It was this embodiment of the Jewish tradition, the Jewish religious tradition—a Torah scroll. If one thinks of the secular Chaim Weizmann giving, and the Baptist Harry Truman receiving, a Torah scroll, one sees a number of themes.

The author Lewis Carroll once said, "It's a poor sort of memory that only works backward." On the contemporary Israeli calendar, two days follow one another within a week—Holocaust Remembrance Day and Israel Independence Day. So within a short time span, a symbolic couplet is formed in the Jewish consciousness—depths of despair to redemption. There is even a program called The March of the Living where both American and Israeli teenagers are brought to the concentration camps to visit Auschwitz and Birkenau and see the depths of the Holocaust—what it cost the Jewish people. Following the visits to the camps they are reinvigorated in their sense of what the establishment of the State of Israel actually means. If we are going to be responsible in remembering the past with an eye towards the future, and if we are to come to terms with the enormity of what the transformation caused by the establishment of the State of Israel has meant for the Jewish people, we need to tell ourselves a number of different stories.

Perhaps the worst pathologies generated in human experience are the result of our ability to focus on only a single narrative—our own narrative—which is devaluating and dismissing of the narratives of others. The key to a more positive future, a future that will heal the torn fabric of the world we all inherit, is for us to attune ourselves to hear a variety of narratives other than our own. Here then are a couple of the narratives that we have to hear.

It was not an accident that the Torah was the central symbol that Weizmann, a secularist, would give to a Baptist president. One central narrative transformed by the establishment of Israel is a religious narrative. The State of Israel, established in 1948, is not the first Jewish commonwealth or the second Jewish commonwealth. There were two prior Jewish commonwealths. The first ended with the destruction of the temple in the sixth century BCE. The second Jewish commonwealth, to all intents and purposes, was destroyed by the Romans in 63 CE. From that time, Jews lost their religious connection to their state. This was not trivial, because during the time of the first commonwealth, a major religious transformation took place. What had been groups of random tribes living in a relatively disorganized and fragmented way, were centralized during the seventh century BCE. At the same time, Jewish worship was standardized and centralized at the temple in Jerusalem. This was a great transformation, as described in the Bible; however, this transformation bore a heavy price. Because Jewish religious life came to be focused on the temple in Jerusalem, imagine the level of the tragedy when the temple was destroyed and the religious state, as people had come to know it, was no longer possible. This created a practical problem: How do you maintain a community without a center of worship?

The destruction of the temple in 63 CE also created a profound philosophical and theological problem: the problem of theodicy. If you are worshipping a God who is supposed to be just and good, how could God have permitted the destruction of his temple and his people to take place? From the destruction of the second commonwealth in the first century CE, in a time when both rabbinic Judaism and Christianity were created, a variety of approaches came about to explain how such a tragic thing could happen. Jews and others have struggled to explain how a just God could allow this kind of devastation to take place, especially if Jews were supposedly a chosen people (a difficult concept in itself). Remember that couplet, "How odd of God to choose the Jews?" But, if in some way, the Jews were chosen, how could they be subjected to this degradation and to this terrible loss? Obviously a theological problem. Various schools of thought sought to identify the sinfulness of the Jews. Later, in rabbinic Judaism, the loss of the temple and homeland was ascribed to ethical decline—people were no longer freed of hatred for one another and this generated the catastrophe. The whole concept of exile and explanation for exile became a fundamental theme in Jewish history and Jewish religious thought. The narrative of decline, of exile, of catastrophe and tragedy, has been transformed in modern religious circles. The establishment of the State of Israel is often referred to as *reshit t'zemichat ge'ulatenu*, the beginning of the flowering of our redemption. If the ultimate degradation and punishment was the Holocaust, then the establishment of the State of Israel is not just an historic event, it must be a transforming event in God's world, theologically, cosmologically, and historically, on the broadest possible map available. This historical narrative is now embodied in our Jewish liturgy, in our literature, in our culture.

The Holocaust was not simply part of a religious narrative; it was, in a sense, a culmination of an extraordinary historical odyssey for the Jewish people. Those who have studied Jewish history in the traditional way see a series of tragedies, one catastrophe following another catastrophe, one pogrom following another pogrom, one expulsion following another expulsion, one campaign of murders following another forced conversion, and so on. The story is not inaccurate, but it is only partially accurate. One Jewish historian has described this kind of telling of the Jewish narrative as "a terrible distortion." While he agreed that no one could deny that the catastrophes have taken place, and that the record of Jewish survival is a record stained with blood, generation after generation and country after country (what he called the lacrimosal, the tearful, conception of Jewish history), this approach excluded the entire history of Jewish creativity. Set beside the murders and the pogroms and the expulsions and the forced conversions and the inquisitions, the extraordinary record—from the time of the fall of the Second Temple—of Jewish creativity in religious literature and in secular literature, in poetry, in drama, in law, in lore, and theology is often forgotten. Of course, this narrative underwent radical change with the establishment of the State of Israel. The Holocaust wiped out nearly all of Jewish scholarship in the world; at that time, American Jewish institutions were only beginning to flourish, and they were all served by the products of Jewish institutions in Europe. The State of Israel had not yet been established and Hebrew University was only beginning to occupy a significant place. With a single merciless blow, the entire course of Jewish energy and creativity was nearly wiped out.

If it had not been for the establishment of the State of Israel, there would be no Jewish community. There is no reason to expect that the Jewish people could survive the Holocaust in any meaningful way with all of its intellectual, academic, spiritual, and religious leadership destroyed. It is one of the miracles of the modern Jewish experience that today, in the twenty-first century, there is more outstanding Jewish scholarship and creativity in the world, both in the State of Israel and in the United States. Now, even European Jewish communities, which phoenixlike have arisen from the dead, again occupy an important place in Jewish history. All this could not have been achieved without the establishment of the State of Israel. It is not that all Jewish scholarship takes place in the State of Israel, but without the center of energy radiating from the State of Israel, the Jewish community would lack that central source of energy and leadership necessary for a viable community.

When I say listening to a variety of narratives, I am aware that even those I have just referred to are not unproblematic. For example, I had a conversation with a young great-niece the other day. She is going to have a bat mitzvah this coming summer. She lives in the Washington area and she called me up because she has to give a talk at her bat mitzvah ceremony. She has to talk about the portion of the Torah called Va-etchanan, the second portion in the book of Deuteronomy, which contains both the Ten Commandments and the Shema. She was troubled because she knows the story about Moses not being admitted to the Promised Land, and she was thinking about this story. She said, "Do you think it's fair that Moses couldn't come to the Promised Land?" Furthermore, she said, "While I'm talking about that, do you, Great Uncle, think that it's fair that the Israelite conquerors of the Promised Land displaced all those who were in the Promised Land before?" I could not say that was fair. My response was, "There are many things in our scripture, in our Bible, that are not there to make us feel better but to make us feel alert and concerned."

We face this same issue in terms of our contemporary narrative. For Jews, the creation of the State of Israel is a remarkable, transforming re-emergence of Jews on the stage of history. It is a miraculous occurrence in Jewish history. However, we must be attuned to the narrative of those for whom this is not a great triumph, of those who feel displaced, who feel that they are being made to pay the price that the European community ought to pay for the Holocaust. We do not have to accept that narrative, but we cannot pretend that there is not justice and understanding and reality to that narrative. In fact, unless we can hear that narrative and understand that narrative, just as we ask that our Muslim and Arab friends understand the narrative of what the State of Israel means to Jews, there is no possibility that we will ultimately reach a peace in the Middle East.

I talked about the photograph of Weizmann and Truman with the sacred Torah. Unfortunately, religious symbols and religion are not providing, in our world, the kind of hope as an instrument for healing that religion should supply. Part of the problem is that religions tend to speak in terms of exclusive access to truth and exclusive access to virtue. As soon as we make claims of having exclusive truth on our side, then we dehumanize the other. We place others into a lower category. We must be able to find a way of hearing our own narrative, whether it is a religious narrative, or a political narrative, or a cultural narrative, in a manner that does not devalue the other. We must hear the narrative that may be different from our own and be sensitive to it rather than be threatened by it. This is the only possible key for a transformed and redeemed world.

I want to close by describing a practice that we do at our Seder table. At the traditional Seder table, we drink four cups of wine, two before the meal and two after the meal. In Jewish tradition, the number four is a significant number, particularly on Passover. The Bible uses four verbs to talk about redemption and departing the land of Egypt. However, in traditional Jewish style, there is a debate about whether there should be five languages of redemption—requiring a fifth cup of wine. So being compromising, our resolution is that we drink four cups of wine, but there is a fifth cup of wine that is placed on the table and called "Elijah's cup." It contains the symbolism of what Elijah represents in Jewish tradition. Elijah heralds the coming of the Messiah, that is when the time of transformation comes, it will be announced by the coming of Elijah as the herald. There is no question that in terms of the religious narrative, the historical narrative, the cultural narrative, and the spiritual narrative, the establishment of the State of Israel represents *reshit t'zemichat ge'ulatenu*, "the beginning of the *t'zmechat* of the flourishing of our redemption." But it is only the beginning.

It is a mistake to deafen our ears to other narratives, because then we doom the world to go back into the depths of despair rather than moving it towards redemption. Around our table, we mark that by not filling Elijah's cup from the bottle of wine. We take the empty cup and we pass it around the table, and each person pours from his or her cup of wine into the cup of Elijah, representing each person's part in that redemption.

It is appropriate that we pause to celebrate, to reflect, to remember. We may also honor the distinguished American who is clearly a Jewish hero for what he did. He was responsible for remarkable transformation. We celebrate that, but this is not the place where we want to rest. In tribute to Harry Truman, and in tribute to the best that is within each of us, we have to look upon this world and say, this world that was torn apart is a world that needs repair and needs healing. In this age, there are some who would like to simply look up high and say, "Well, it will come by some divine intervention."

This is not going to happen unless each of us contributes to that process of repair and healing.

So when we pour those drops of wine into the cup of Elijah, we are saying, "Let us rededicate ourselves in the spirit of Harry Truman, in the spirit of the best in our tradition and in all traditions. Let us commit ourselves, in genuine tribute to what has been accomplished, to the repair and healing of the world. Let us do our share to bring about that true redemption so that Israelis and other peoples, neighbors of Israel and others around the world will witness together with us, not simply the *reshit t'zemichat ge'ulatenu*, not simply the beginning of the flowering of our redemption, but a worldwide redemption in its full flowering."

Islam and the Quest for Peace in the Middle East

Ahrar Ahmad

Assalamu alaikum. While 75 percent of the world's Muslims are not Arabs, that particular Arabic expression is the universal greeting used by all Muslims everywhere. In the spirit of this conference, I should also point out that the traditional Jewish greeting is *Shalom aleichem,* and in the old Latin church the usual greeting was *Pax vobiscum.* What is most interesting is that all three greetings mean essentially the same thing: May peace be upon you. One of the most delicious and dangerous ironies of history is that while the great faiths have talked peace, and taught peace, greeted peace, and fêted peace, unfortunately many of the faithful have not. They are more apt to say, "My religion is the religion of justice and compassion, mercy and love; therefore, I hate you."

In today's world of transitions and contradictions, that particular irony has gained surprising and poignant salience. On the one hand, there is no doubt that the world has become much smaller than it used to be thirty years ago. Trade and tourism, cultural contacts, informational resources, and emerging technologies have figuratively and literally put the world at our fingertips. But, while the forces of integration have been so powerful, the forces of disintegration, on the other hand, have been no less compelling. Today we see unprecedented levels of violence and conflict in the world, divided as it is along lines of caste and class, tribe and race, language and culture, region and religion.[1] The last is the most counterintuitive (because education, democracy, and human progress are expected to decrease such tensions) and has the most far-reaching consequences. And, to be honest, a great many current misgivings in the world today surround the religion of Islam. Let me address at least some of those issues with the intention of clarifying some misconceptions that confuse and divide us. I am particularly concerned about those stereotypes popular in the West (e.g., Islam is undemocratic, regressive, unjust, violent, and intolerant of other religions) that are considered to present insurmountable obstacles to securing a fair and durable peace in the Middle East, particularly in the conflict between the Palestinians and Israelis.

Is Islam (which literally means "submission to the will of God") inherently hostile towards Judaism and Christianity? Let me first point out that it is most impressive that the phrase "Judeo-Christian tradition" has acquired such wide legitimacy and popular currency. If those two faiths could overcome the deep and bruising scriptural and historical divisions that they have to contend with, it is entirely possible that Islam—much closer to either of them than they are to each other—can also be incorporated as part of that same tradition. Islam situates itself deliberately and self-consciously as part of a continuum in the evolution of the monotheistic faiths, not as a rupture but a completion, not a challenge but a culmination of a process that may not necessarily have begun with Abraham, but was dramatically shaped by him. Hence we find the centrality of Abraham in the narrative of the three faiths, as a common ancestor to all of them, both spiritually and genealogically.[2] He has left us a rather messy will, but that is our problem, not his.

But, instead of giving you some high-sounding rhetoric about the essential unity and humanity of all people, let me indicate to you precisely what the Quran—the Holy Book of the Muslims—says about this, and related matters.[3] The reason I am quoting from the Quran is that it is considered to be the supreme authority for Muslims, the text that informs and inspires their entire existence, and which contains the exact and inerrant words of God that no Muslim can violate or change. To avoid misunderstanding, it is better that I quote from it directly than that I provide paraphrases and assertions. I would like to point out that I am using the Quran for evidence and argument, as a scholar's tool, not a preacher's weapon.

In chapter 29 verse 46, the Quran explicitly states, "And dispute you not with the People of the Book [i.e., Jews and Christians] but say, 'We believe in the revelation which has come down to us, and in that which came down to you, our God and your God is one, and it is to Him we bow in Islam.'" Islam accepts the prophethood of Moses and Jesus (and others mentioned in the Tanakh and New

Testament), accepts the stories contained therein (Adam and Eve, Noah and the ark, Jonah in the whale, Sodom and Gomorrah, etc.), accepts almost all the miracles and stories attributed to Moses and Jesus (the parting of the waters, the burning bush, the miraculous birth of Jesus, the curing of lepers, the raising from the dead, and so on). As a matter of fact when Muslims take the name of the prophet Muhammad, they say parenthetically, as a mark of reverence to him, "May peace be upon the Prophet." And when they take the name of Moses and Jesus, they say exactly the same thing. There is no doubt that both of them are revered as God's chosen messengers. However, Islam contends that it is possible that the books revealed to them, in human hands, gradually evolved in ways that could have compromised their original purity. It should be pointed out that, contrary to popular opinion, the Quran *never* refers to believing Jews and Christians as "infidels." The Quran tells us, "We believe in Allah, in what has been revealed to us, what was revealed to Abraham, Ismail, Isaac, Jacob, and the Tribes, and what was imparted to Moses, Jesus, and the other prophets from their Lord, making no distinction between any of them, and it is to Him we submit" (2:136 and 3:84). In a similar vein, and more explicitly, the Quran states, "Those who believe in the Quran, and in the Jewish scripture, and the Sabians and the Christians, who believe in God, and the Last Day, and work righteousness, on them shall be no fear nor shall they ever grieve," a refrain that is repeated in exactly the same language in two different chapters in the Quran (2:62 and 5:72).

But isn't Islam opposed to the other religions? Well, the Quran reminds the faithful that God has sent messengers to all the nations (16:36, 10:47), that all prophets, some mentioned by name in the Quran and some who are not (4:164), are bearers of divine law, teachers and reformers, engaged in similar ministries, and those who believe in them "and make no distinctions between them, will receive their just rewards" (4:152). Their messages and good tidings were to ensure that "humanity may not have a plea [or argument] against God" (4:165). The Quran itself proclaims that "if [Allah] so willed He could have made us all one people" (5:51) but He did not, and made us into various nations and tribes, with these diversities themselves representing a sign from God (30:22). These differences extend beyond physical characteristics, and the Quran asserts that "to each among you we have established a law and an open way," not to engender discord and confrontation but "so that we may know each other and not despise each other" and compete in excelling each other in virtue and piety (5:51, 49:13). Even though Islam presents itself as the final expression of God's messages, it suggests, quite categorically, that "there is no compulsion in religion" (2:256), and holds out the possibility that not all will submit to the teachings of Islam or commit to its message. Thus, the while Quran indicates that the truth has been conveyed, and it would be a mistake to deny the messages and signs from God contained therein, it adds, "let who will accept, and let who will reject" (18:29). While it proclaims that it presents the "straight path" to God, it does not specifically claim that it is the only one. There is a pluralist expansiveness evident in chapter 109, entitled "the Unbelievers," where the entire chapter of six lines is dedicated to only one message instructing Muslims to say that "ye will not worship what I worship, nor will I worship what ye worship...to you your way, to me mine." Consequently, the sweeping generalizations in the West that present Islam as a relentlessly finger-wagging, deliberately exclusivist, and angrily self-righteous religion (stereotypes that, admittedly, some Muslims help to reinforce), go against the grain of Islamic principles in terms of the revelations contained in the Quran.

But isn't Islam incompatible with democracy? The religious coexistence I referred to earlier hints at Islam's commitment to democracy—democracy not as a set of institutions and procedures, but in terms of its substance and spirit, what some scholars refer to as "deep democracy."[4] In this context, the concept of consensus becomes relevant. Chapter 42 verse 38 indicates that those people are dear to God "who conduct their affairs by mutual consultation." While some conservative scholars interpret this as consultation only among a select group of advisors, family members, or the *ulema* (the learned ones), the chapter itself indicates no such limitation. In fact, in chapter 3 verse 159, it is suggested that Muslims should try to forgive and pray for those who may have been weak in faith and judgment and "consult even them in affairs of the moment." Hence, there is no test of virtue or intellect that limits the franchise or restricts the people from participation. Moreover, the Quran emphasizes the significance of human will as a transforming instrument. The faithful are reminded in chapter 13 verse 11 that "verily never will God change the condition of a people unless they want to change it themselves," thus suggesting that the believers are not supposed to be passive or timid recipients of the ruler's dictates, serving merely as objects of history, but should be engaged participants and active agents in the betterment of their lives and communities.

But isn't there a lot of injustice in Muslim countries? Perhaps, but that would be inconsistent with the foundational tenets of Islam. The Quran exhorts the faithful to "stand out firmly for justice, as witnesses to God, even as against yourself, or your parents, or your kin, or whether it be against rich or poor (for God can protect both). Follow not the lusts of your heart, lest you swerve, and if you distort justice or decline to do justice, God is acquainted with your deeds" (4:135). The believers are supposed to be absolutely honest and fearless in their understanding and administration of justice, not even sparing or showing partisanship to their families and kin. Therefore, the argument (or the excuse really) that Muslims cannot condemn some acts of wanton brutality committed by some wayward Muslims because, after all, they are Muslims, is inconsistent with Quranic doctrine. In fact, the Quran enjoins the believers to make sure that not even their anger or anguish or hatred can make them act inequitably. "Be just," the Quran reminds us, "for that is nearer to piety" (5:9).

But isn't that legalistic concept of justice rather indifferent to social inequality and oppression? The widely shared perception of Islam is that it is defined purely by some legal and ritual commitments, and that as long as some of these rules (or pillars) are followed, Muslims are assumed to be on the right path. However, the Quran tells us that "it is not righteousness that we turn our faces towards the East or West" in prayer, but that we fulfill our responsibilities to our community through helping the vulnerable and by meeting our contractual obligations (2:177). The Quran asks, "Hast thou observed him who believeth faith? It is he who repels the orphan and urges not the feeding of the needy" (107:1–3). In chapter 51 verse 19, the Quran suggests that in the wealth of the rich "the beggars and the needy have their due share," thus indicating an entitlement rather than a mere dependence on the charity of others. God's favor and grace are always intended for the poor and oppressed among us, and most of the prophets (with some exceptions) came from among them as leaders and inheritors (28:5). God's anger is not necessarily directed against the rich, because, after all, wealth and success can also indicate God's generosity, but is leveled at the vanity, the arrogance, the ostentation, and the selfishness that the rich are wont to demonstrate, particularly those "who pileth up wealth, and spend it not in the way of the Lord" (104:2–4 and 9:34). Indeed, the weak and distressed are encouraged to challenge the illegitimate and unjust rulers "who oppress humanity with wrongdoing, and insolently transgress beyond bounds through the land defying right and justice" (42:42). The pomp and power that some kings and noblemen may display could disappear quickly if, through their oppression, they incur the displeasure of the people, and the wrath of God. The Quran warns: "And how many townships have we destroyed while it was oppressive, so that it lieth to this day in ruins, and how many a deserted well and lofty tower" (22:45). As the prophet Muhammad so famously said, "O Lord, I seek refuge in Thee from poverty, scarcity, and indignity, and I seek refuge in Thee from being oppressed and from oppressing others."[5]

But isn't Islam inherently violent? There is no doubt that Islam permits, indeed encourages, robust retaliation against those who unjustly initiate war against the faithful. However, it also reminds us, "Fight in the way of Allah those who fight you, but do not begin hostilities, for God likes not the aggressors" (2:190). In typical biblical tradition, it accepts the argument of appropriate punishment, but adds, "The recompense for an injury is an injury equal thereto, but if a person forgives and makes reconciliation, his reward is due from the Lord" (42:40). This theme of forgiveness extends even to groups in conflict with the Muslims, those who may cease and desist from oppression or violence, or offer peace or surrender, or wish to extend their hand in friendship. No conflict is permanent, except against oppression and injustice, and the Quran reminds the believers that "it may be that God will grant love [or friendship] between you and those whom ye now hold as enemies" (60:7). Therefore, opportunities for reconciliation between contending parties should never be foreclosed and the Quran suggests, "if the enemy incline towards peace, do thou also incline towards peace, and trust in Allah" (8:61). For those who do not fight the believers on account of their religion, or do not make it impossible for them to practice their faith, or do not turn them out of their homes, the Quran encourages the Muslims "to be generous to them, and deal with them justly" (60:8). While bravery in the battlefield, for a just cause, is glorified, the Quran also suggests that "If anyone slew a person (unless it is for murder or spreading corruption) it would be as if he slew the whole people, and if anyone saved the life of a person, it would be as if he saved the life of the whole people" (5:35). War is never a first choice for Muslims, but the last alternative they may be forced to follow, but which they must undertake if it is thrust upon them. The Quran tells us, "Know that Allah is with those who restrain themselves" (9:36), and that the faithful should be fully aware that they are supposed to be "a community in the middle way so that (with the example of your lives) you might bear witness to the truth before all mankind" (2:143). Indeed, in chapter 5 verse 31, the Quran counsels the faithful: "If thou stretch thy hand to kill me, it is not for me to stretch out my hand to kill thee, for I fear Allah." And, in referring to the sacredness of all life, it suggests that no life can be taken except "by way of justice and law" (6:151, 17:33). A pithy admonishment probably captures the gist of Islamic teaching rather well: "Cultivate tolerance, enjoin justice, and avoid the fools" (7:199).

But doesn't the Quran provoke the believers to "slay the idolaters wherever you find them"? It does, in chapter 9 verse 5. But perhaps it should be pointed out that this is specifically in reference to the Meccan pagans who have broken treaties and acted in unfair and aggressive ways. And it should be remembered that in the very next sentence—in the same verse—the Quran says, "but if they repent, and establish regular prayers, and practice regular charity, then leave their way free." And following that, the next verse advises that "if one of the pagans ask thee for asylum, grant it to him, so that he may hear the words of God, and escort him to security" (9:6). The same expression, "slay them," also occurs with reference to those who persecute (2:191). However, the very next verses suggest "but if they cease…let there be no hostility except against the oppressors" (2:192–93). And again, in chapter 4 verse 89, the words "slay them" recur in the context of those who lead the Muslims astray from their faith and turn into renegades. But immediately after, it says, "if they withdraw from you and fight you not and (instead) send you guarantees of peace, then Allah has opened no way for you to war against them" (4:90). We must bear in mind that taking a word or phrase out of the Quran without reference to the framework of the narrative, or the ethos of the faith, is both misleading and unfortunate.

Is it possible that I myself am using the Quran selectively to present the idea of a progressive Islam that is inconsistent with popular stereotypes? Perhaps. But I am convinced that I am presenting the essence of Islam accurately and honestly. It is true that one can read into the scripture whatever one wants. Every act of reading is a textual deconstruction, every act of understanding, an interpretation. What you read into a text is what you bring to it, and want from it. If you want to find peace, justice, and compassion in the Quran, you can, as you can in most sacred texts. If you want to discover anger, hate, and violence in the Quran, you can do that too, as you can in most sacred texts. It is most curious, and probably sad,

that some who hate Islam, and some Muslim fanatics, are both reading it in the latter way.

I must point out that the undemocratic regimes we see in most
of the Muslim majority countries, and their awkward embrace of
modernity, are there not because of Islam, but in spite of it. The tur-
bulence, bigotry, and bloody-mindedness that some Muslims are
demonstrating in some parts of the world can probably be analyzed
from the perspective of economic uncertainties, political alienation,
and the cultural dislocations they are facing. These conditions are
ripe for manipulation by self-righteous and self-appointed leaders—a
task made easy for them by the low level of Quranic literacy in most
of these countries. I humbly submit to you that it is not their scripture that is leading some Muslims to anger and frustration; it is their
perception of powerlessness and injustice that is driving them to
their scripture in strange and perverse ways. We must try to understand the context before we condemn the text.

The common ground that I think the religions share is not
merely theoretical, expressed in some stray scriptural flourishes, but
it has also been demonstrated in specific historical moments. The
Prophet of Islam lived with Jews and Christians, dealt, traded, trav-
eled, married, and had contractual and personal relations with them.
Actually, the only son born to Muhammad after he began receiving
the revelations (and who was named Ibrahim or Abraham) was born
of his Christian wife. Admittedly, there are some examples of his
frustration with Jews and Christians, but there are innumerable
other illustrations of his tolerance and acceptance, such as his inclusion of the Jewish tribes within an interfaith corporatist structure in
the Medina Charter of 622, his dealings with the Christians of Naj-
ran, or his gratitude to the Christian king of Abyssinia for saving the
Muslims from persecution, among many such instances.[6]

It is interesting that periods of high Muslim rule (the Abbasids
from the eighth to the tenth centuries, Islamic Spain from the tenth
to the fifteenth centuries, Ottoman rule from the fifteenth to the
mid-seventeenth centuries, and Mughal rule in India from the mid-
sixteenth to the late eighteenth centuries) presented tantalizing possibilities. During these periods, we find efforts towards the establishment of the rule of law and robust discussions regarding different
juristic interpretations that led Muslims to develop several equally
acceptable jurisprudential schools. We also find relatively rational
bureaucratic structures, the incorporation of other groups into a tol-
erant social milieu, and administrative systems that included not just

People of the Book, but also others (for example in India) who were not. We also find the encouragement of scientific learning, aesthetic refinement, and philosophical debate; indeed, classical Greek writing found its way back into the European lexicon through Arab intellectual mediation.[7] All of these hint at the potentials for democratic and enlightenment ideals that were gradually being expressed therein.[8] It should also be pointed out that some of these possibilities were significantly undermined through the impact of Western imperialism that gradually imposed an exploitative, violent, cynical, divisive, and autocratic rule over most of those areas, sometimes directly or sometimes through indirect manipulation, which caused profound dysfunctionalities that many Muslim lands have yet to overcome.

Finally, I would like to draw your attention to the fact that in the Muslim world, we do not find the kind of vicious anti-Semitism evidenced elsewhere in history. The Muslims did not destroy any Jewish (or Christian) places of worship when they captured Jerusalem in 638; in fact, the Muslim caliph ordered the Wailing Wall area to be cleaned up. It was not the Muslims who inflicted a policy of execution and expulsion on the Jews in Jerusalem in 1099 when the city went under Crusader control; in fact, Saladin invited them back after he recaptured the city in 1187. The Muslims did not evict the Jews from Spain in 1492 (where they had lived in particularly harmonious amity); in fact, it was the Muslims who welcomed them into the Ottoman Empire, where they were allowed legal autonomy and spiritual jurisdiction over themselves. It should be pointed out that by the seventeenth century almost 30 percent of the population of Istanbul was Jewish and that they were there by choice, not by conquest or coercion.[9] And, obviously, there is nothing comparable in the Muslim world to the culture of paranoia, disdain, and exclusion that Jews faced throughout most of their history in the West, which eventually found extreme and tragic expression in the brutal eliminationist ideology that emerged in some parts of Europe in the twentieth century. None of this implies that all Jews and Christians who lived under Islamic rule enjoyed absolute peace and justice. Surely there were bitter misunderstandings and savage encounters between Muslims and the others. But, and this is my point, these incidents were episodic and determined by circumstance, and were neither systematic nor governed by doctrine.

My argument, indeed my hope, is simply this—there is both scriptural space and historical example for Muslims and Jews and Christians to try to live in just and peaceful coexistence, as they have, even in the Middle East. Their history may have been complex and troubled, but not inherently conflicted, nor their future necessarily doomed. What I see today, with much anguish and anxiety, is that an essentially political contest between Israelis and Palestinians over land, water, resources, boundaries, rights, sovereignties, security, etc.—all quantitative problems hence negotiable and solvable—is gradually becoming a religious conflict that is not negotiable or solvable. It would be naive of me to pretend that religion has nothing at all to do with this tragic confrontation. But it would be mischievous of me to propose that the issues we face there today are necessarily, or even primarily, religious in nature (except, perhaps, the status of Jerusalem, which demands more delicate handling than our leaders have so far demonstrated). Further, even on some sensitive issues where religion cannot be ignored, there is no reason why the last sixty to seventy years of misunderstanding and turmoil should overwhelm or subvert a much longer tradition of tolerance and historical interaction between the Jews and Muslims, or why the voices of generosity and forgiveness that their respective religions profess should be silenced by the shrillness of the unjust and the selfish that their respective religions decry.

Whether we construct the dreadful "other" out of each other and make it into a self-fulfilling prophecy, or whether we have the wisdom and grace to accept each other and live out our common destinies, whether we have the famous clash of civilizations, or a dialogue of civilizations, whether it is here in America or there in the Middle East, it is up to us. I would just like to remind everyone that every dead Palestinian child and every dead Israeli child is testimony to the failure of our collective will, proof of the foolishness of our ways, indeed evidence of the betrayal of our faiths. My friends, *assalamu alaikum*—May peace be upon you.

Notes

I would like to thank Drs. Omar Farooq, Shahid Alam, Christine Shearer-Cremean, Jeff Chuska, Mr. Nisar Amin, and Mrs. Hasina Ahmad for their suggestions and support. None of them is responsible for the ideas or language contained herein. A version of this speech was delivered at the Network of Spiritual Progressives conference at the University of California, Berkeley, on July 23, 2005.

[1] This point is well developed in Benjamin Barber, *Jihad vs. McWorld: How Globalism and Tribalism Are Reshaping the World* (New York: Ballantine Books, 1966).

[2] Even though Bruce Feiler's book (*Abraham* [New York: Harper Collins, 2002]) is breezy and journalistic, it effectively pursues the hypothesis of common claims that all the three religions make on Abraham.

[3] All Quranic references in terms of chapter and verse are from Abdullah Yusuf Ali, *The Holy Quran: Translation and Commentary* (Lahore: Islamic Propagation Center, 1934). In a few instances, for clarity or expressiveness, I have also used the translations of Mohammad Marmaduke Pickthall, *The Meaning of the Glorious Quran* (New York: Mentor Book, n.d.); and Majid Fakhry, *An Interpretation of the Quran: English Translation and Meanings* (New York: New York University Press, 2004). There are no differences in meaning or interpretation. A related clarification may be necessary. It is customary, though not absolutely required, for Muslims to attach the acronym *"saw"* which, in Arabic, means "peace be upon him," if a prophet's name is mentioned, and *"swt"* which translates as "the most glorified and exalted," if God's name is used. These invocations are implicit throughout the essay.

[4] The concept of "deep democracy" is suggested in Judith Green, *Deep Democracy: Community, Diversity and Transformation* (London: Rowan and Littlefield, 1999). See also Joshua Cohen, "Procedure and Substance in Deliberative Democracy," in Seyla Behabib, ed., *Democracy and Difference: Contesting the Boundaries of the Political* (Princeton, NJ: Princeton University Press, 1996); and Phillipe Van Parijis, "Contestatory Democracy vs. Freedom for All," in Ian Schapiro and Casiano Hacker Gordon, eds., *Democracy's Value* (Cambridge: Cambridge University Press, 1999), 191–98.

[5] This is from the Sunan of Abu Dawood Book 8, number 1589. I am using the language adopted in Asghar Ali Engineer, *Religion and Liberation* (Jawahurnagar, Delhi: Ajanta Publishers, 1989).

[6] The full text of the Declaration of Medina is available in Abdulrahman Abdulkader Kurdi, *The Islamic State: A Study Based on the Islamic Holy Constitution* (London: Mansell Publishing House, 1984). It should be pointed out that the arrangement with the Jews broke down after a while in some confusion and bloodshed. But it was due to external and contextual factors, not because of a conflict over faith or practice.

[7] For this specific point, see Joel Kramer, *Humanism in the Renaissance of Islam: The Cultural Revival during the Buyid Age* (Princeton, NJ: Darwin Press, 1985), 3; Franz Rosenthal, *The Classical Heritage in Islam* (London: Routledge, 1975), 14; and Glenn Perry, *The Middle East: 14 Islamic Centuries,* 3rd ed. (Saddle River, NJ: Prentice Hall, 1997), 77.

[8] This argument is made in much greater detail in Ahrar Ahmad, "Islam and Democracy: Text, Tradition, History," *American Journal of Islamic Social Science* 20, no.1 (Winter 2003): 29–35.

[9] See Robert Mantran, "Foreign Merchants and Minorities in Istanbul," in *Christians and Jews in the Ottoman Empire: The Functioning of a Plural Society*, ed. Benjamin Braude and Bernard Lewis, 127–38, esp. 128 (New York: Holmes and Meier Publications, 1982); and Christopher de Bellaigue, "Turkey's Hidden Past," *The New York Review of Books* 48, no. 4 (March 2001): 38.

ENVISIONING PEACE BETWEEN ISRAELIS AND PALESTINIANS

William A. Brown

In 1979, I stumbled into United States–Israel relations as the number two man at the U.S. Embassy in Tel Aviv. I worked for a great ambassador, Sam Lewis. During this period after the Camp David Peace Accords, the withdrawal of Israeli forces from the Sinai, the Israeli air force's bombing of the Iraqi nuclear reactor, and Israel's 1982 invasion of Lebanon all took place. In this context, I dealt with Ariel Sharon, then Israel's agricultural minister and the head of the water authority. My first introduction to him was via Ezer Weizman. Ambassador Lewis sent me over on a courtesy call to the defense minister. As we talked, a shadow—a large shadow—moved by, and Ezer called out, "Arik, come on in here. I want you to meet Bill Brown." And in came Ariel Sharon, with a great roll of blueprints and plans under his arm. These were the plans of the settlements that he was planning to build in the months ahead. And, since I had come to meet with him in that capacity, he gladly rolled the plans out for me and told me exactly what he was going to do. It was mind-boggling. In those days, there were about seven or eight thousand settlers on the West Bank. There are now a quarter million. He laid the plans all out very openly, no surprises.

In those days, we in the American Embassy in Israel were forbidden to be in the West Bank. The United States government did not want Embassy personnel to be seen on the West Bank. This was because our presence there might be misinterpreted as American

On January 5, 2006 (six months after this speech was given), Ariel Sharon suffered a massive stroke that left him in a coma and permanently hospitalized.

recognition of what was going on there, that is, the building of settlements. Nevertheless, I drove my own car up to a site called Ariel and I saw the bulldozers moving around. I said to myself, "Wow! This is mind-boggling! This is not being constructed for a small group of Israeli pioneers. This is being constructed for thousands." Today there is a city of many thousands up there, with swimming pools, an auditorium, a university, and other amenities. In those days, Ariel Sharon was the settlement king.

In the later 1970s and into the 1980s, when Sharon was in various government positions, when he was defense minister during the Israeli siege and bombardment of Beirut in 1982, he and I went head-to-head. After I was named U.S. ambassador in 1988 (as a Reagan appointee and a career officer), I dealt with him as minister of commerce and industry (1988–91), as minister of housing later on, and later as minister of development. We had many lively conversations. In fact, I would say that before he became prime minister, I probably had more dealings with Ariel Sharon than did any other American diplomat. Maybe that is an exaggeration, but I certainly had a lot to do with him. I always used to tell stories about Sharon, to the shock of my liberal Israeli and American friends, because they had a stereotype of him as an awesome, threatening, bulldozing individual. He is a subscribing member of the Israeli Symphony Orchestra and he plays the violin. This would shock them; they didn't want to hear that because it didn't fit with their image of Ariel Sharon. Once, shortly after he became defense minister, my wife, Helen, and I were invited down to his farm. We had a wonderful time riding around his farm. Sharon was already the greatest farmer in Israel. His melons, vegetables, and fruits were being exported to Europe, and he employed an Arab shepherd who managed a thousand head of sheep. I kept wondering all day long, "Why am I down here? What does he want?" Eventually I found out: he wanted a trip to Washington, DC, to meet the United States leaders as the Israeli defense minister. That's what he wanted.

The question for us in 2005, now that Ariel Sharon has been prime minister for several years, is: How capable is he of the transformation necessary to achieve a lasting peace with this Palestinian entity? It's a big question with no easy answer. I will tell you, Sharon has a remarkable spectrum of experience—in war, settlements, industry, commerce, and highways. This is an extraordinarily intelligent man with wide-ranging experience. Whether he can bring himself, with the disengagement from Gaza, to the next step, leading to final status negotiations, is a major question. Is disengagement from Gaza an attempt solely at unilateral action for U.S. and European public relations benefits, perhaps some minor adjustments to the disengagement plan for "coordination"? Then, perhaps there will be withdrawal from four small, distant settlements in the northwest of the West Bank, thereby presenting a de facto situation? Is the plan to withdraw from Gaza, but then consolidate the major Israeli settlements near the green line, along with an expansion of greater Jerusalem? If that's the case, we're all in trouble over the long term.

We need significant American engagement. I've gone all over that map questioning what the Israelis and the Palestinian Arabs each want for themselves. I'm back to square one. Without heavy American involvement, a permanent solution probably won't happen. This is not just the problem of Sharon: it is the problem of Sharon and the Palestinians, with the hard-line Israelis and the hard-line Palestinians, the extremists on both sides. There must be American involvement at the highest level in order to provide the moral, economic, and political push on both sides.

Abu Mazen, the head of the Palestinian Authority, has a long history with Sharon. I do not claim that Abu Mazen is a moderate; however, he has consistently called for a nonviolent, negotiated approach. He now presides over a situation in Gaza that is absolutely chaotic. I remember my own trips there ten years ago and how dangerous it was. The situation now is much more troublesome as a result of the latest intifada. Hamas, with its extremist position and its suicide attacks on Israel, has scored great victories. It enjoys the prospect of being elected to significant seats, perhaps even a majority, in the Palestinian Authority. Can we negotiate with them? This remains to be seen; but if there is going to be progress, we need United States involvement. Let's hope that we see really serious American involvement.

I was dead set against the invasion of Iraq. I'm an old Marine. I'm of an age where my old Marine Corps colleagues are deluging me with e-mails that show how brave our Marines in Iraq are, and how well they're performing, along with all of the U.S. military forces. I fully accept and appreciate their bravery and heroism, and our government's good intentions. However, what bothered me from the beginning was the initial mistake of invading Iraq (now remember, I'm a veteran of Saddam Hussein's scuds). In my view, Iraq was nothing but an oil-dominated, oil-motivated entity. It was a

Kosovo, with a problematic combination of Sunnis and Shiites who are religiously opposed to each other, and Kurds who are vehemently opposed to both groups. My concern was that if you topple this thug Saddam Hussein, what would be gained in the end?

Just as the Israelis tried to impose their kind of government in Lebanon, and failed for various reasons, it remains to be seen whether we can impose a kind of Western-style democracy on a totally alien Islamic culture in Iraq. We've now lost more than 1,600 American troops and many, many thousands more have been wounded. The carnage goes on. I keep hearing that the corner is about to be turned; I hope it's true. However, I remain concerned that what we may see is the continuation of this violent insurrection and deterioration into an open religious war between the Sunnis and Shiites, with the Kurds poised to declare their independence at any moment. That development—Kurdish independence—would bring in God knows how many other actors, including the Turks, Iranians, and Syrians. The invasion of Iraq has created a dangerous situation.

I am the proud, unpaid chairman of the board of the Harry S. Truman Research Institute for the Advancement of Peace. This institution is in Jerusalem under the wing of the Hebrew University, and is supported by the American Friends of Hebrew University. The Hebrew University of Jerusalem, a wonderful university, was founded by Albert Einstein, Chaim Weizmann, and others back in the 1920s. In 1965, a group of Jewish American supporters of the Hebrew University visited Harry Truman at his home in Independence to ask permission to use his name for a memorial or an institute in Jerusalem. Truman, in essence, let these visitors know that he didn't want to go down in history only as the man who dropped the bomb. He wanted to be remembered in history as the man who struggled for peace. So he said, "If you want to open an institute in my name, make it the institute for peace." They said, "Of course, Mr. President," and went on their way. According to my oral sources, as they left the former president's home they looked at each other and said, "What in the world is he talking about? What's an institute for peace?" Elihu Elath, who in 1948 had been the first Israeli provisional government representative in Washington and was now the head of the Hebrew University, said, "Of course, we can do it."

Truman liked the plan for the institute and got behind it. President Lyndon Johnson sent Thurgood Marshall, the prominent black U.S. solicitor general about to be named a Supreme Court justice, to

Commemorative stamp issued by Israel in 1975. Israelis continue to remember and honor the U.S. president who recognized their country at the vulnerable moment when it was first proclaimed and desperately needed friends. (Truman Library)

Jerusalem for the groundbreaking. It was a great event. Unfortunately, the whole thing went sour temporarily because the entourage around Harry Truman had envisaged an institution up on the Mount Scopus campus totally independent from the Hebrew University. The donors to the new Institute, however, were also backers of the Hebrew University, and they prevailed; the Truman Institute for Peace moved ahead. In the 1970s, in a very dangerous, courageous move, Institute staff extended their hands to Palestinian scholars in private meetings. In the context of their time, it was a radical thing to do, and they were subjected to severe public criticism. Nevertheless, they said, "Isn't there a way we can resolve this to the benefit of both of our peoples?" There are now several remarkable examples of cooperative endeavors, and I'd like to briefly discuss some of them.

The Oslo breakthrough took place in 1993, at the time of Yitzhak Rabin. Things looked hopeful then, and staff at the Truman

Institute for Peace set about joint studies with Palestinian scholars. One of those studies addressed the tremendously explosive issue (then and now, and in the future) of water, which is terribly scarce for both the Israelis and the Palestinians. The major Palestinian population lives on very rich land from which flows the waters that Israel uses. Israeli control of water in their occupation of the West Bank has been absolutely firm and rigid. One cannot drill a well without Israeli permission. As both Israeli and Palestinian populations have expanded, control of water has emerged as a highly volatile issue. The Truman Institute backed Israeli hydrologists and persuaded Palestinian counterparts to sit down and produce a joint study. This document was published, but unfortunately, it has been forgotten because of the intifada. However, the problem of water will not go away and its solution will be painful for both sides. But it has got to be done.

In another example of a cooperative effort, the former rector of the Hebrew University, Yehoshua Ben-Arieh, published (through the Truman Institute) a remarkable pamphlet on a proposed trilateral land exchange between Israel, the Palestinian Authority, and Egypt. The basic problem behind this land exchange is that Gaza is too small to support its population. It now has 1.3 million people, and there are few resources there. Gaza is overpopulated, underresourced, and in absolute chaos. Ben-Arieh argues that the Gaza land area has to be expanded, and that if the Egyptians would give the Gaza strip an extension on the Egyptian side the additional land could lead to the prospect of development, with significant external aid. He suggests compensating the Egyptians with a small chunk of the Negev, which would give them the right to achieve a long-held desire—a road that would link Egypt to Jordan, providing a valuable commercial connection. The third part of the deal would have Palestinians yield portions of the West Bank that would enable the Israelis to keep their settlements right along the green line. This is the kind of creative thinking that is needed these days as we look ahead to solving difficult challenges.

I was once standing on the roof of the power generator at Ashdod with the plant manager who knew that I was an environmentally focused ambassador who had worked in the EPA. And he knew what I was after. I wanted to know what sort of emissions were being put out and how they were being handled. He said, "Well, the way we do it is this. We burn the heavy stuff at night, so the people can't see it. Because I don't have the money under the

Israeli electric authority to put in the necessary filters." I said, "Where does it go at night?" He said, "Well, the breeze changes. It depends. On certain days it goes that way, out towards the Mediterranean and Europe. On other days, it goes that way, toward Jerusalem and the Palestinian Authority." The burning of crude oil at this plant immediately affects the Palestinian Authority and Jerusalem as well. There is a lesson here. If the situation is left unchanged, the effect on both sides of each other's actions can be enormous, just in the environmental area of air pollution.

In addition to conferences and studies, the Truman Institute for Peace conducts polls of public attitudes held by both Israelis and Palestinians. A recent poll demonstrated some good news and some bad news. Here's the good news. In March 2005, 84 percent of the Palestinians and 85 percent of the Israelis polled supported a return to negotiations on a comprehensive peace settlement. Despite their individual preferences, 53 percent of the Israelis and 51 percent of the Palestinians say they will support their leadership's decision to proceed with the peace process, even if it's by a route they don't personally agree with. Thirty-nine percent of the Palestinians and 60 percent of the Israelis polled support the current "road map." Seventy percent of the Israelis and 59 percent of the Palestinians believe that it's possible to reach a compromise settlement with the other side's current leadership. Forty-eight percent of the Israelis believe that Israel should negotiate with Hamas, if necessary, in order to reach a compromise agreement. Think about that. Hamas is characterized by Israel's government and by the United States as a terrorist organization. Yet 47 percent of the Israelis polled now believe that they should negotiate with Hamas. Doesn't this make sense on a very basic level? Whom do you negotiate with? Your enemy, of course.

Israelis and Palestinians have entirely different views on why Camp David failed. According to the poll, 63 percent of the Israelis believe the main reason is that the Palestinians were not forthcoming and continued to use violence. Only 5 percent of the Palestinians polled believed that. Fifty-four percent of the Palestinians put the blame mainly on Israel for not being forthcoming and for continuing to build settlements. Fifty-two percent of the Israelis support and 44 percent oppose a referendum on Sharon's disengagement plan. Sixty-seven percent of the Israelis support dismembering most of the settlements in the territories if that's what is needed. Interestingly, 75 percent of the Palestinians see Sharon's plan to evacuate the settlements in Gaza as a victory for the Palestinian armed struggle. Most

Israelis find this view extremely troubling.

Polls indicate that Israelis and Palestinians believe in democrati-zation, and both groups believe in American policy involvement. Fifty-five percent of the Israelis and 79 percent of the Palestinians believe that the United States should increase its involvement in try-ing to solve the Israeli-Palestinian conflict. General support for rec-onciliation among Israelis has also increased, and stood at 84 percent in the 2005 poll compared to 80 percent in 2004. In 2005, 81 percent of Palestinians supported reconciliation, compared to 67 percent a year before. Fifty-five percent of the Israelis and 89 percent of the Palestinians polled in 2005 will support open borders and free move-ment of people and goods after a comprehensive settlement. Seventy percent of the Israelis and 73 percent of the Palestinians support joint economic institutions and ventures. Fifty-one percent of the Israelis and 13 percent of the Palestinians will support the adoption of the school curriculum that recognizes the sovereignty of the other state and educates against irredentist aspirations. In 2004, 41 percent of the Israelis and only 4 percent of the Palestinians were willing to support this. Clearly, there remain strong feelings among the Pales-tinians against the possibility of a joint school curriculum that pro-motes these positions. That's bad news. But that's precisely what we at the Truman Institute are about, and we need to address Hamas. In addition, we've got to educate both the Israelis and Palestinians and their children to accept a new mind-set.

I enjoyed a series of very interesting conversations with Prime Minister Yitzhak Rabin following the completion of the Oslo Accord. He called me to his office to tell me privately about the Accord. The agreement shook Washington because it came about without Washington's participation. When Rabin met with me, he said, "Bill, this is what happened at Oslo and I want you to promise me not to report to Washington yet, because Shimon Peres is flying now to meet with Secretary of State Warren Christopher. Peres will lay it all out when he arrives." I said that it would be kept secret, and then he laid out the Oslo segment for me. Oslo had taken us all by surprise.

In the U.S. State Department, we knew of meetings in Oslo and we even knew that there was a scholar from the Truman Institute, Ron Pundak, among those meeting in Oslo. Of course, we didn't know the scope and seriousness with which things were going; once Washington learned what had happened, I was instructed to go immediately to see Rabin and extend an invitation to him directly from President Clinton. The president wanted to meet with Rabin to announce this great breakthrough he had nothing to do with bringing about. So I went to Rabin and we met one-on-one. He sat there with his cigarette and offered me a cup of Turkish (or as the Arabs would say, Arab) coffee. As Rabin sat down, I said, "Mr. Prime Minister, I have the honor to extend an invitation to you personally from President Clinton. He asks that you meet with him and Yasser Arafat in Washington to commemorate this great breakthrough." Rabin took a puff on his cigarette and said, "Ah, Bill. There's no business like show business."

Rabin invited me on his plane and we flew together to Washington. I well remember being in the capital for a day of euphoria. At least American liberals and progressives were euphoric. At the public event, kids were wearing green shirts reading "Seeds of Peace." It was just magnificent.

Unfortunately, as a professional, I was very conflicted. I walked from the ceremony on the White House lawn over to the State Department, where I sat down and handwrote a letter to the secretary of state. I noted that Rabin had just taken a very courageous, even dangerous, move. I recommended a recognition of this and—as an American effort to push the whole thing further—I recommended immediately moving our embassy to Jerusalem. I believed we had to move ahead aggressively on what had been authorized by the Accord. I felt strongly about the move of the U.S. Embassy from Tel Aviv to Western Jerusalem as a symbolic gesture. However, I knew when I wrote my report that there was no hope of it being done at the time.

Once, when calling on Prime Minister Begin, I used the expression "return to the status quo." Begin was a highly educated man and proud of his excellent command of Latin, as well as English, French, Hebrew, Yiddish, German, and Russian. He said, "Bill, status quo is the wrong expression. Some situation is either the status quo or it is not; there is no status quo to which we can return. Perhaps it is the status quo ante that you are referring to, a return to how things were." That was a lesson for me, linguistically and otherwise—one important lesson among many that I got from Menachem Begin. The status quo in any situation is constantly changing. In the Israeli-Palestinian struggle, we want neither the present status quo nor the status quo ante. In the Middle East, we must strive for a peaceful resolution that creates a new order of things, a new status quo.

APPENDIX A
The View from the White House
An Interview with George M. Elsey

Michael T. Benson

George M. Elsey served both presidents Franklin D. Roosevelt and Harry S. Truman in various administrative capacities. A graduate of Princeton and Harvard and a trained historian, Mr. Elsey first came to Washington, DC, as a naval aide in the early 1940s. In the Truman White House, he was an assistant to Clark Clifford, the president's White House counsel, and later administrative assistant to the president. Given Mr. Clifford's dramatic and pivotal role in the American recognition of the State of Israel—including his famed May 12, 1948, showdown in the Oval Office that pitted the young Clifford against the venerable General George Marshall—he was asked for an on-camera interview to record his remembrances of the Palestine episode. However, due to ill health, Mr. Clifford was unable to grant such a request. In his stead, he recommended Mr. Elsey for his intimate knowledge of the details and events of 1947–48.

BENSON: When President Roosevelt died in April of 1945, what was the feeling in the White House?

ELSEY: Roosevelt's death and Truman's sudden ascendancy to the presidency shocked the public at large far more than it did people in Washington, DC. Senator Truman had established a superb record as chairman of the War Investigating Committee.[1] He was very well-known on Capitol Hill and throughout the executive branch.

Interview conducted December 4, 1997, in Washington, DC, by Michael T. Benson. Edited by Robert Kirschner for the Skirball Cultural Center Los Angeles, California.

While people said, "Who is this guy? He's totally unknown," that wasn't at all true. He had been featured on the cover of magazines such as *Time* and *Newsweek* and credited widely for his performance. He was regarded as one of the two or three most important men in Washington. The public at large was startled, but those in business and in government were well acquainted with the man.

But Truman knew darn little about some of the most sensitive issues that he would soon have to face, because FDR had not taken him into his confidence. Some things, such as the Manhattan Project[2] he knew absolutely nothing about until a few hours after he became president....

BENSON: When Truman assumed office, he inherited Roosevelt's Middle East policy. How did his position differ from FDR's?

ELSEY: Truman began his first days and weeks in office by assuring everyone that he was going to follow President Roosevelt's policies. This was a general statement to reassure the nation, and the world for that matter, that there were not going to be any sharp deviations. It was a way of avoiding some of the more difficult decisions that he was [unintelligible] them to one side: "We'll take care of that after the war." President Roosevelt had been specific in meeting with King Ibn Saud[3] of Saudi Arabia upon returning from the Yalta Conference. He assured Ibn Saud that the United States would not do anything in the Middle East without full consultation with the Arabs. That was a commitment that Admiral Leahy[4] made sure President Truman knew about almost immediately. But from all the pressures he was getting from all sides, Truman realized that he was going to have to make some tough decisions pretty soon, decisions that were bound to upset some people.

BENSON: Where did the Palestine issue fit on Truman's list in the critical year of 1948?

ELSEY: The early months of 1948 were some of the toughest of Harry Truman's presidential years. He was being hit by all sides, domestically and internationally. On the world scene, Palestine was very much on his mind. He was aware that the British Mandate would soon be ending—his Jewish friends in this country would never let him forget what their problems were. He had to keep in mind, though, that we were facing critical problems in Europe on the continent. In March, the Soviets took over Czechoslovakia to the shock and the horror of the Western world. We were so weak, militarily speaking, all around the world that Truman went to Congress and asked for the reinstitution of selective service, a difficult matter and a horror to the country to think that so soon after we demobilized we were going to have to go back to possible mobilization again.... There were problems in Germany: the Soviets began the first Berlin blockade—this was a short one, it didn't last—but it was a precursor to the big blockade that began later that year. Finland was under great pressure. It signed, on its knees, a defense agreement with the Soviets which made many people fear that Finland might suffer the fate of Czechoslovakia. The Norwegians appealed to the United States and England; they too were under pressure from the Soviets....

A year earlier, Truman had gone to Congress and asked for aid to Greece and Turkey to combat the Communist threats there, but it was a long, long way from solving those problems. The Communists still had the upper hand in most of the Balkan Peninsula. Italy was teetering. Italian elections were coming up in April of '48, and it appeared that the Communist Party had a good chance of pulling off a victory—they didn't, it was a very, very narrow thing. Europe was not the only place that worried us. South Korea was under pressure. In China, Chiang's[5] forces were beginning to fall apart, and just a few months later, he had to flee with his forces to Formosa [Taiwan].

Of great concern to the military was not only our weakness in manpower but the instability in the Middle East. Uppermost in the minds of the Army and Navy was whether we could maintain access to Middle Eastern oil. While President Truman was feeling very sympathetic to the necessity of having a homeland for the Jews, he had to bear in mind also what he was hearing constantly from throughout the executive branch: Don't do anything that will lose us our access to Arab oil. So, these were the things hitting Truman twenty-four hours a day, seven days a week, in those early months of '48.

Of course, I haven't said a word about the domestic situation. The [Republican-controlled] Eightieth Congress was riding high, passing bill after bill that [Democrat] Harry Truman had to veto and then see his vetoes overridden. His famous civil rights message of February '48[6] was splintering the Democratic Party, leading to the establishment of the Dixiecrats. He was at sea on whom he would want to run with him as vice president in the forthcoming campaign, assuming he could get himself renominated. So here was a guy under pressure and occasionally he blew his stack.... Who wouldn't under the circumstances?

BENSON: To support Jewish aims in Palestine, Truman had to contradict the State Department, people like Dean Acheson[7] and George Marshall[8], Robert Lovett[9], and Dean Rusk.[10] How do you explain his position?

ELSEY: To fully understand Harry Truman's position on the Palestine question and homeland for the Jews, I think we have to go all the way back to the man's boyhood. He read the Bible, he studied the Bible, he knew the Bible well. He had grown up with just a basic feeling within him of the rightness of a homeland for the Jewish people. This was reinforced, as it was in the minds of most people everywhere, by the horrors of the Holocaust. It just reinforced what he had always believed, that the Jewish people had a right to a homeland. Almost every other national group had a nation of its own, but not the Jewish people, and they deserved one....

Truman took into account, listened, and understood, the advice of the State Department on the importance of not doing anything in the Middle East that would lose us the working relationships with the Arabs and might open a way for further Soviet penetration into the area. In that sense, the State Department's position was almost identical with that of the secretary of war and the secretary of the navy. So Truman was not siding specifically against the State Department; he was in effect taking on the whole political-military establishment when he decided to move in a pro-Israel direction, specifically the immediate recognition of the State of Israel when its creation was announced.

BENSON: What was your perception of Zionist pressures on the White House?

ELSEY: President Truman was subject to pressure on many, many issues. The Zionist pressure was perhaps as intense as any. It came from people like Chaim Weizmann[11] It came from senators and congressmen who sometimes were Jewish themselves or had substantial Jewish constituencies. It came from within his own White House staff, namely, from David Niles,[12] one of the few carryovers from the Roosevelt administration. And it came in the form of mail: vast quantities of mail addressed to the president, much of which he could not see simply because of the pressures of time and space. But he got it from all directions.

BENSON: How do you account for Clark Clifford[13] becoming the advocate within the White House for the establishment of the State of Israel?

ELSEY: In the well-known and now famous episode in the Oval Office at the White House, when Clark Clifford and General Marshall clashed so directly over the question of whether or not the State of Israel should be promptly recognized, Clifford was simply doing what Harry Truman had asked him to do: make the case for immediate recognition. Clark Clifford was a lawyer, and Harry Truman was his client. Clifford was serving his client to the best of his ability....

BENSON: You've mentioned the tension in the spring of 1948, as the Palestine situation came to a head. One of the crucial moments was the meeting on May 12, 1948. Clark Clifford, in his memoirs, calls it the showdown in the Oval Office. Tell us about that.

ELSEY: I was waiting in Clifford's office when he came back from the showdown meeting in the Oval Office. He was very distressed at the [divisive] turn it had taken. He outlined to me what had happened, and said, "We've got to work our way out of this." We talked back and forth, and I said, "I think that Undersecretary Lovett is going to be the key to this." Obviously the same thinking was going on over in the State Department, because just about that moment, the phone rang and it was Lovett calling Clifford saying, "We've got to get together and see how we can work our way out of this situation." Clifford agreed to go to Lovett's house for a talk. Later Clifford and I discussed it again, and he kept me posted. In fact, I spent most of the next couple of days in his office....

I regret very much that Clark Clifford is not able to speak to you today. His health has not been good. When I described this project to him, he told me how deeply he regretted he could not participate for reasons of health. He regards his role in helping President Truman carry out his policies with respect to Israel as among the better things that he did for Harry Truman. He believes that this was one of Harry Truman's most courageous acts as president, and he asked me to carry that message on.

BENSON: At the May 12 meeting, historical accounts tell us that Marshall threatened to break with Truman. He said that at the next election, if he were to vote, he would vote against the president. What would have happened had that statement become public?

ELSEY: It was essential that there not be an open break, a public break with General Marshall, secretary of state. Marshall had a reputation that was unsurpassed in our country at that time. It took his personal prestige to get the Marshall Plan [to rebuild the shattered European economy] through the Congress.... Truman, after all, was an unelected, accidental president in the eyes of many people, and if a man like Marshall were to walk away from him, even the possibility of Truman's renomination would be in doubt. There would have been questions: Does the United States have a foreign policy, and if so, who's running it? Do we have a man who's not capable in the White House? I hate to think about the implications of what would have happened had there been an open break between Harry Truman and George Marshall.

BENSON: How is it that Truman was willing to oppose someone like George Marshall on the partition issue?

ELSEY: President Truman was a very courageous man. When he believed something was the right course, he would take that course regardless of the brickbats that he knew would be coming in his direction. He was convinced in his heart that the Jewish people deserved a homeland. The State of Israel was about to come into being. He was determined to let the world know that he believed the State of Israel should exist and should be recognized. It was a conviction on his part, an act of conscience.

BENSON: For years now, some people have argued that Truman recognized Israel as quickly as he did because he needed two things: Jewish political support in influential states like New York and Jewish money. What is your response to these allegations?

ELSEY: In February of '48, just three months earlier, Harry Truman sent his civil rights message to Congress: the boldest, bravest message on civil rights that any president had ever sent to the Congress. It laid out the ground rules for the debate on civil rights in this country for the next thirty years. Would you say that he was just doing this for the black vote? No, he did it because he believed it was the right thing to do, despite the consequences. And one of the consequences, in the case of civil rights, was the defection of a large part of his party—the Democratic Party. I think there's a degree of comparability here. He did what he knew was right. Sure, there were some political advantages to it, but there were enormous disadvantages.

In the case of the recognition of Israel, there were some political advantages, but there were a great many negatives as well. In both cases, he was doing what he believed was the right thing for the nation, for the American people....

BENSON: What was the response to Truman's immediate recognition of the State of Israel?

ELSEY: Astonishment, shock, surprise. The American delegation at the United Nations was so flabbergasted that in the first few minutes after word hit Lake Success, where the UN was then sitting, that the United States had announced recognition of the State of Israel, our delegates went around denying that it had happened because they couldn't believe it. And this same sense of shock was apparent in newspapers around the world the next day. Zionists were overjoyed. The British and a number of others were upset. The Middle East was generally in turmoil. The Arab countries, of course, felt that they had been double-crossed because this was contrary to what they thought the American position was going to be.

BENSON: How would you rank Truman among American presidents?

ELSEY: When Truman left office in January of '53, his public ranking was very low indeed. It has risen steadily as the nation and the world have come to realize the significance of decisions that his administration made and executed, including the Truman Doctrine,[14] NATO, the Marshall Plan, civil rights, recognition of the State of Israel, and the desegregation of the armed forces. These are decisions that are now recognized as significant landmarks in American history. So Truman's rating is high. I don't think it's fair or appropriate to try and say number one, two, three, four among our presidents. Each president has to deal with the issues of his time and his day. Some deal successfully with them, others evade making decisions and don't accomplish much. Truman was a good president, and we now generally regard him as a great president, because he faced up to the issues and made decisions.

I think this is a point about Truman's ability to make a decision. He didn't equivocate, he didn't waffle, he didn't keep pushing things off. This was one of the first things noted by those cabinet officers who remained in office after Roosevelt's death: the difference between FDR and Harry Truman. They would leave FDR's office not really being sure just where he stood, whether he agreed or disagreed. But nobody ever left Truman's office without knowing where Harry Truman stood. They might not have liked the decision he made, but they would darn well know what it was.

BENSON: Was Truman proud of his decision to recognize Israel?

ELSEY: I wouldn't say that Harry Truman was proud of his decision. I'm objecting to the word "proud." There wasn't pride in the man. He didn't pat himself on the back for having done things or having made decisions....

Back to the analogy with civil rights: all the political figures on [Capitol] Hill and elsewhere who were consulted when Truman was preparing the civil rights message in February '48 said, "Oh my God, you can't do that this year!" They recognized that it would cause great consternation in the Democratic Party, particularly in the South, and in their view the Democrats could not hope to win the election without a solid South. But that didn't stop Truman; he went right ahead with it. When Congress paid no attention to his civil rights message, he did the only thing that he could do within his own right and issued two executive orders, ending segregation in the armed forces and in the civil service. He did that against the opinion of a substantial number of political leaders.

This was a guy who did what he believed was right, regardless of what others said. "Oh, you can't do that; that's too dangerous; don't, don't, don't." That didn't stop Harry Truman.

Notes

[1] War Investigating Committee: While the official title was the Senate Special Committee to Investigate the National Defense program, it was known as the Truman Committee almost from its inception. The committee began its work on April 15, 1943, and was charged with the task of investigating the awarding of defense contracts. Estimates vary as to exactly how much money the committee saved the U.S. government during World War II, but its work is recognized as one of the most successful congressional investigations in American history.

[2] Manhattan Project: The code word assigned to the development of the atomic bomb. In early 1943, investigations from the Truman Committee had been picking up puzzling hints of a secret enterprise that was commanding huge, unexplained expendi-

tures. Secretary of War Henry L. Stimson, who preferred to call the project S-1, briefed President Truman fully for the first time on April 25, 1945.

[3] King Ibn Saud: The king of Saudi Arabia, King Ibn Saud met privately with President Roosevelt on Great Bitter Lake, midway through the Suez Canal, shortly after the Yalta Conference on February 14, 1945.

[4] Admiral William D. Leahy.

[5] Chiang Kai-shek: Leader of the Chinese Nationalist government forces that were defeated by the Red Armies of Mao Tse-tung. Chiang Kai-shek and his followers were forced to seek refuge on the island of Formosa.

[6] The Civil Rights Message of February 1948 was the strongest civil rights message ever enunciated by an American president. Among its major points were a federal law against the crime of lynching, more effective statutory protection of the right to vote everywhere in the country, a law against poll taxes prevailing in seven states of the Old South, an end to discrimination in interstate travel by rail, bus, and airplane, and an order to the secretary of defense "to take steps to have the remaining instances of discrimination in the armed services eliminated as rapidly as possible."

[7] Dean Acheson served as undersecretary of state and later as secretary of state in the Truman administration. While Acheson and Truman shared similar perspectives on a wide range of global issues, Palestine was one area on which their attitudes dramatically diverged. Acheson wrote that he had learned to understand, but not share, the mystical emotion of the Jews about returning to Palestine. American Zionists, according to Acheson, had allowed their emotion "to obscure the totality of American interests."

[8] George Marshall was army chief of staff during World War II and later secretary of state in Truman's cabinet and Nobel laureate. His opposition to President Truman's support of the State of Israel came from his military background and his belief that the Jews in Palestine had no chance of withstanding the invading Arab enemies.

[9] Robert Lovett served as undersecretary of state to General George Marshall and later secretary of defense. Considered one of the establishment "Wise Men," Lovett played a key role in persuading Marshall not to oppose President Truman publicly over the Palestine issue.

[10] Dean Rusk served as assistant secretary of state in charge of United Nations affairs. General Marshall dispatched Rusk to New York after Truman's immediate recognition of Israel on May 14, 1948, in order to prevent the American delegation to the United Nations from resigning *en masse* in protest against the president's action.

[11] Chaim Weizmann was the distinguished spokesman for the international Zionist movement and later the first president of the State of Israel. Through efforts of Truman's former business partner, Eddie Jacobson, Weizmann met with the president in March 1948 to discuss the urgent need for American support of the nascent Jewish state.

[12] David Niles served as President Truman's assistant for minority affairs. Though naturally self-effacing with a preference for anonymity, Niles was a persistent pro-Zionist voice in the sea of anti-partition advisors surrounding Truman.

[13] Clark Clifford was a young Missouri lawyer who began his White House service as a naval aide in 1945 and later became special counsel to President Truman at age forty. At critical junctures throughout the entire Palestine episode, Truman relied heavily on Clifford's advice and on his ability to articulate the president's pro-partition position.

[14] On March 12, 1947, President Truman delivered a speech to a joint session of Congress, spelling out what became known as the Truman Doctrine, which asserted that it was "the policy of the United States to support free peoples who are resisting attempted subjugation by armed minorities or by outside pressures."

Appendix B
My First Forty-five Minutes with Harry S. Truman

Abba Eban

I believe a nostalgia for leadership inspires very many people when the name of Harry S. Truman arises in their minds. My first encounter with President Truman lasted for forty-five minutes and it made a profound impression upon me. I learned more in those forty-five minutes about President Truman, about his style, about his temperament, about his manner of expression than in all the subsequent years.

It occurred to me that I was sitting only a few yards away from the most powerful leader in the history of mankind, more powerful than the Babylonian and Persian emperors, than Alexander the Great, than Julius Caesar and Napoleon, than the rulers of the British Empire at its zenith, than the Russian and German dictators of the twentieth century. So here was I, a very young ambassador all of thirty-two years old, of a still younger country.

There had never been a time when one nation held such predominance of military and economic power as did the United States on the morrow after the Second World War. America had attained that primacy during a conflict in which all of the other participants had suffered defeat or devastation or exhaustion, or all three of them together. After the war, the United States had a monopoly on

Drawn from remarks made by Ambassador Abba Eban at a symposium sponsored by the Harry S. Truman Library Institute at the Library of Congress, October 25, 1995. Abba Eban was Israel's first ambassador to the United Nations, and from 1950 to 1959 he served simultaneously as ambassador to the United States and to the United Nations. Ambassador Eban's first visit with President Truman was September 5, 1950, in the Blair House.

nuclear weapons; it created 50 percent of the world's product, and it dominated the voting systems in all the newly established international agencies. Of course, in the traditional centers of diplomacy in Paris and in London, the governments of France and Britain might secretly believe that their experience and wisdom transcended the naive perceptions of American statecraft. But politics is principally about power—it is not principally about wisdom or experience. And in terms of power, even Britain and France had to recognize that America had no real competition.

So, the man whom I faced at the other side of the table held the ultimate decision in the deployment of overwhelming power. And, as I looked at Harry Truman, I wondered if power had ever been expressed with such total absence of pretension or pomp. He was about five feet nine inches tall, square shoulders, a long sharply edged nose, steel rimmed spectacles. The White House was undergoing repairs. Blair House was the house in which he would spend most of the seven years of his incumbency. The air conditioner was much more well-meaning than effective, and the presidential countenance was bathed in perspiration. His jacket was missing and his increasingly soggy white shirt was framed by suspenders of a stark red hue. If you passed him on the streets of a small town, you would imagine that he was on his way to a little office in a moderately sized building. If there was such a thing as the imperial presidency, nobody had broken the news to Harry S. Truman of Independence, Missouri.

The occasion for my encounter was the presentation of credentials as ambassador of Israel to the United States. Obedient, therefore, to the chief of protocol in your State Department, I had dressed in formal clothing with the conventional silver gray tie, and bore with me the bulky documents wrapped in leather, containing the letters of credence which would assure President Truman that I really was who I purported to be—namely the ambassador extraordinary and envoy plenipotentiary of the State of Israel to the United States of America. I confess that I was prepared for a more elegant and formal encounter. I had heard from my colleague the Israeli ambassador to London of the way in which he was transported to the royal presence by six horses of identical pedigree and shape, driving across the streets of London and leaving those streets in a rather disagreeable condition. The credentials are rarely noted for literary grace or innovation.

It was evident the president was afraid of something. He feared that I might follow tradition and actually declaim the text. In order to preempt that danger, he snatched the documents from my hands and said, "Let's cut out the crap and have a real talk." He then cast a triumphant glare at the disconcerted chief of protocol, who had prepared me for a much more elegant ritual. It was already plain to me that President Truman regarded his own State Department as a hostile foreign power.

The president's first inquiry to me was a deferential question about the health of my president, President Chaim Weizmann. This illustrated his tendency to see international politics in strictly human terms. President Weizmann had captivated Truman with his tact, dignity, and precision while the president was totally alienated from the official Zionist leadership. Now this caused us, and especially me, delicate problems. Real power in Zionism lay no longer with the deposed elder statesman, but with Abba Hillel Silver, the reigning chief of American Zionism, and with David Ben-Gurion, who was the undoubted leader of Palestinian Jewry. But Truman regarded Silver with severe aversion, regarding him not inaccurately as a supporter of the Republican Party, which came second only to the Soviet Union as a primary target of President Truman's distrust. Truman was quite indifferent to Ben-Gurion's qualities and met him only once during his presidency. It was quite useless to tell him that there were new leaders in Zionism. Truman seemed to believe that if you were president of the United States, you could decide with whom you would or would not hold discourse.

Once, in March 1948, when there was a crucial need to prevent a defection of American support from the idea of Jewish statehood, when only direct access to the president could achieve this aim, the Zionists had to bring the aged Weizmann, in a querulous mood, thousands of miles across the ocean. Even then, it had not been easy to secure the interview because Truman was firm in his refusal to have contact with any Zionist leader, suspecting them of what he called "emotionalism." In a handwritten note to a White House aide, he had included Arabs and Latin Americans in this accusation, adding a prayer to God that "the children of Israel would get an Isaiah and the Christians a St. Paul while the Arabs would get some insight into the Sermon on the Mount." It was possible to get Weizmann into Blair House on that occasion only if we allowed Harry Truman's former business partner, Eddie Jacobson, to persuade Truman that Weizmann corresponded in Jewish history to President Andrew

President Harry S. Truman accepting a gift from Israel Prime Minister David Ben-Gurion in a meeting on May 8, 1951. Standing behind them is Israel Ambassador to the United States Abba Eban. (TL 59-1584-02)

Jackson, whose portrait heroically adorned the president's office. Jacobson asked me if it was permissible for me to put those two historical figures in the same light. I told Jacobson that, as a student of history, I believed that no two human beings had ever walked on earth with fewer common attributes than Andrew Jackson and Chaim Weizmann. I added that since the establishment of a Jewish state was for me a much higher interest than historical accuracy, I was prepared to join the preposterous Jackson-Weizmann analogy for the sake of what I thought was a greater good.

When I surrendered my credentials and reported on Weizmann's health and mood, our "crapless" conversation took its course for forty minutes. Truman made no claim to rhetorical distinction. His sentences flowed without any expectation that his voice or formulation would rise even spasmodically above the solid flat farming earth in which he was nurtured. But there was never any difficulty in grasping the core of his thought. He said twice that the decision to drop the atomic bomb on Hiroshima and Nagasaki had caused him no anguish and no discomfort. Now, this was startlingly irrelevant and he had created no context of relevancy. I was no more than an ambassador, very young, fulfilling his formal duty. But, from Truman's allusion, I deduced that his anguish and discomfort must have been intense. He warned me again to beware of striped-pants boys in the State Department, staring reproachfully at the striped pants of the hapless chief of protocol. From this charge he exempted only Dean Acheson. "Dean does what he thinks I want and even pretends to like doing it. In addition, he has enough brain power for two dozen ordinary men."

I deduced from this experience that Truman's greatest gift lay not in expression, but in decision, and in decision his courage and independence were exemplary. He never hedged or waffled. He would never support opposing contingencies in order to claim rectitude with any result. The list of his epoch-making decisions is extraordinary. He *decided* to drop the bombs on Japan. He *decided* to force Soviet troops out of Iran. He *decided* to assume the responsibilities which Britain had abandoned in Greece and Turkey. He resolved to offer Marshall aid to western and eastern Europe. He resolved to accept East Europe's rejection with serenity. He *decided* to establish the North American Treaty Organization. He *decided* to contain Soviet expansion. He *decided* to resist North Korean invasion of South Korea. He *decided* to dismiss General MacArthur for insubordination. He *decided* to despise Senator McCarthy of Wisconsin in strident terms. And he *decided* to recognize Israel, thus fixing the parameters of the postwar Middle East. And finally, he *decided* to fight his successful election campaign which at the time he seemed to have no chance of winning.

In his recognition of Israel, he had total solitude of decision. Everybody else was against it. George Marshall was against it. John McCloy was against it. George Kennan, to my regret, I think now to his regret, was against it. Dean Rusk was against it. Loy Henderson was against it. None of his supporters except Clark Clifford was really ready to give his backing. There was a sort of historic imagination that was at work in Truman, and he had the impression that the foreign policy of the United States was run by the president of the United States. It is impossible not to withhold respect for this assertive use of the presidential power and for his unexpected success in securing domestic consensus in its behalf.

Surely the conclusion must be that Harry S. Truman influenced the direction of his nation's life more profoundly than any of his successors, many of whom earned more contemporary adulation. The Truman presidency, it seems to me, is the constitutive period in the modern international system. It was then that most of the vocabulary and conceptual habits of American thinking on international politics over most of the past fifty years became firmly embedded in the western consciousness with the central themes of activism, responsibility, a large vision of America's place in the world, and a particular emphasis on the vocation of America to be the exemplar and protector of democracy as a universal cause to be defended against external menace and domestic assault. The idea of activism within an enduring coalition, with Western Europe as its central pillar, could not be taken for granted when the Second World War came to an end. It was, as it seemed to many of us then, a sharp deviation from historical experience and from some of the inborn prejudices of the United States. Truman may be said to have established those themes so firmly that no successor ever felt moved to challenge them. During the Truman era, the links of the United States to an alliance system were institutionalized so heavily that the option of a return to normalcy and isolation was effectively eliminated.

I would end by saying that the revisionist school which describes this epoch as a story of missed opportunities for coexistence has not made its case. It is hard to imagine how Truman could have told the American people that he did have a way of bringing the war with Japan to a speedy end but that he had renounced it in favor of some ethical inhibitions. It is hard to imagine how the Soviet Union, haunted by its tragic memories, would ever have renounced its attempts to surround itself with a belt of subjugated countries. It is even more difficult to conceive how the United States could ever have accepted the doctrine that Soviet security could be carried to a point at which it was held to transcend the security of everyone else.

With all of his knowledge about the world and his own place in its future, Truman was utterly immune from the intoxication of summitry, quite unimpressed by ceremonies. Arriving in Potsdam in order to have his first meeting with the rather overpowering figures of Stalin and Churchill, we find him writing to his wife, "I can't get Chanel No. 5. There is none to be had, not even on the black market or in Paris, but I did manage to get some other kind at the American PX for $6. They said it is equal to Chanel No. 5 and sells for $35 an ounce at home, so if you don't like it you can make a profit on it. I seem to have Joe and Winston talking to themselves and both are exceedingly careful with me. Uncle Joe gave a dinner last night. There were at least twenty-five toasts. So much getting up and sitting down that there was practically no time to eat or drink— a very good thing. Being the super duper guest, I suddenly realized that nobody would go until I pulled out, which I did after 11:00 after a wonderful concert."

One day in a meeting with Midwest farmers, he advised them to use more manure, and when a friend whispered to Mrs. Truman,

"Do get him to use the word 'fertilizer,'" she replied, "It took me twenty years to get him to say 'manure.'"

He surrounded himself with men of talent—Acheson, Averell Harriman, John McCloy, Lucius Clay, Clark Clifford, Dwight Eisenhower, Speaker Sam Rayburn, George Kennan—and ruled on a loose rein.

He was much more sentimental than he ever confessed. In 1952, when he had resolved not to seek further office, I eulogized him at a public meeting in Washington and I used the following words: "We do not have orders or decorations. Our country has no tradition of formality or chivalry. Our material resources are small. One thing, however, is within the power of the people of Israel to confer. It is the gift of immortality. Those whose names are linked with our history never become forgotten." As I glanced at him he was wiping away a tear. It was a very far cry from the credentials ceremony.

In January 1953, the architect of these great decisions slipped away from the rather unmemorable Eisenhower inaugural speech, made for the railway station, and chugged his way back to Independence, Missouri. He didn't seem to feel that anything was different. He gathered some friends around him and played cards as he used to do, probably with the same friends.

Nothing much had happened to Harry Truman—except that Harry Truman had changed the world.

APPENDIX C
The Truman Administration and U.S. Recognition of Israel—A Chronology

Raymond H. Geselbracht

1945

August 24: The report of the Intergovernment Committee on Refugees, called the Harrison Report, is presented to President Truman. The report is very critical of the Allied forces' treatment of refugees, particularly Jewish refugees, in Germany.

August 31: President Truman writes to British Prime Minister Clement Attlee, citing the Harrison Report and urging Attlee to allow a reasonable number of Europe's Jews to emigrate to Palestine.

October 22: Senators Robert Wagner of New York and Robert Taft of Ohio introduce a resolution expressing support for a Jewish state in Palestine.

November 13: At a press conference, President Truman expresses opposition to the Taft-Wagner resolution. He says he wants to wait and consider the report of the Anglo-American Committee of Inquiry.

1946

April 20: The Anglo-American Committee of Inquiry submits its report, which recommends that Britain immediately authorize the admission of 100,000 Jews into Palestine.

May 8: President Truman writes to Prime Minister Attlee, citing the report of the Anglo-American Committee of Inquiry, and expressing the hope that Britain would begin lifting the barriers to Jewish immigration to Palestine.

June 21: A Joint Chiefs of Staff memorandum to the State-War-Navy Coordinating Committee warns that if the United States uses armed force to support the implementation of the recommendations of the report of the Anglo-American Committee of Inquiry, the Soviet Union might be able to increase its power and influence in the Middle East, and United States access to Middle East oil could be jeopardized.

September 24: Counsel to the President Clark Clifford writes to the president to warn that the Soviet Union wishes to achieve complete economic, military, and political domination in the Middle East. Toward this end, Clifford argues, they will encourage the emigration of Jews from Europe into Palestine and at the same time denounce British and American policies toward Palestine and inflame the Arabs against these policies.

October 4: On the eve of Yom Kippur, President Truman issues a statement indicating United States support for the creation of a "viable Jewish state."

October 23: Loy Henderson, director of the State Department's Near East Agency, warns that the immigration of Jewish communists into Palestine will increase Soviet influence there.

October 28: President Truman writes to King Ibn Saud of Saudi Arabia, informing the king that he believes "that a national home for the Jewish people should be established in Palestine."

1947

1947–48: The White House receives 48,600 telegrams, 790,575 cards, and 81,200 other pieces of mail on the subject of Palestine.

April 2: The British government submits to the General Assembly of the United Nations an account of its administration of Palestine under the League of Nations mandate, and asks the General Assembly to make recommendations regarding the future government of Palestine.

May 13: The United Nations General Assembly appoints an eleven-nation Special Committee on Palestine to study the Palestine problem and report by September 1947.

August 31: The United Nations Special Committee on Palestine issues its report, which recommends unanimously (all eleven member states voting in favor) that Great Britain terminate its mandate for Palestine and grant it independence at the earliest possible date, and also recommends by majority vote (seven of the member nations voting in favor) that Palestine be partitioned into Jewish and Arab states.

September 17: Secretary of State George Marshall, in an address to the United Nations, indicates that the United States is reluctant to endorse the partition of Palestine.

September 22: Loy Henderson, director of the State Department's Near East Agency, addresses a memorandum to Secretary of State George Marshall in which he argues against United States advocacy of the United Nations proposal to partition Palestine.

October 10: The Joint Chiefs of Staff argue, in a memorandum entitled "The Problem of Palestine" that the partition of Palestine into Jewish and Arab states would enable the Soviet Union to replace the United States and Great Britain in the region and would endanger United States access to Middle East oil.

October 11: Herschel Johnson, United States deputy representative on the United Nations Security Council, announces the United States' support for the partition plan of the United Nations Special Committee on Palestine.

October 17: President Truman writes to Senator Claude Pepper, "I received about 35,000 pieces of mail and propaganda from the Jews in this country while this matter [the issue of the partition of Palestine, which was being considered by the UN Special Committee on Palestine from May 13 to August 31, 1947] was pending. I put it all in a pile and struck a match to it—I never looked at a single one of the letters because I felt the United Nations Committee [UN Special Committee on Palestine] was acting in a judicial capacity and should not be interfered with."

ca. November: A subcommittee of the United Nations Special Committee on Palestine establishes a timetable for British withdrawal from Palestine.

November 24: Secretary of State George Marshall writes to Undersecretary of State Robert Lovett to inform him that British Foreign Secretary Ernest Bevin had told him that British intelligence indicated that Jewish groups moving illegally from the Balkan states to Palestine included many communists.

November 29: The United Nations General Assembly approves the partition plan for Palestine put forward to the United Nations Special Committee on Palestine.

December 2: President Truman writes to former Secretary of the Treasury Henry Morgenthau Jr., encouraging him to tell his Jewish friends that it is time for restraint and caution. "The vote in the UN," Truman wrote, "is only beginning and the Jews must now display tolerance and consideration for the other people in Palestine with whom they will necessarily have to be neighbors."

December 5: Secretary of State George Marshall announces that the State Department is imposing an embargo on all shipments of arms to the Middle East.

December 12: President Truman writes to Chaim Weizmann, president of the Jewish Agency for Palestine and the World Zionist Organization, that it is essential that restraint and tolerance be exercised by all parties if a peaceful settlement is to be reached in the Middle East.

1948

February 12: Secretary of Defense James Forrestal says at a meeting of the National Security Council that any serious attempt to implement partition in Palestine would set in motion events that would result in at least a partial mobilization of United States armed forces.

February 19: Secretary of State George Marshall says at a press conference, when asked if the United States would continue to support partition, that the "whole Palestine thing" was under "constant consideration."

February 21: Eddie Jacobson, a longtime and close personal friend of President Truman, sends a telegram to Truman asking him to meet with Chaim Weizmann, the president of the Jewish Agency for Palestine and the World Zionist Organization.

February 22: President Truman instructs Secretary of State George Marshall that while he approves, in principle, a draft prepared by the State Department of a position paper that mentions as a possible contingency a United Nations trusteeship for Palestine, he does not want anything presented to the United Nations Security Council that could be interpreted as a change from the position in favor of partition that the United States took in the General Assembly on November 29, 1947. He further instructs Marshall to send him for review the final draft of the remarks that Warren Austin, the United States representative to the United Nations, is to give before the Security Council on March 19, 1948.

February 27: President Truman writes to his friend Eddie Jacobson, refusing to meet with Chaim Weizmann, the president of the Jewish Agency for Palestine and the World Zionist Organization.

March 8: Counsel to the President Clark Clifford writes to President Truman, in a memorandum entitled "United States Policy with Regard to Palestine," that Truman's actions in support of partition are "in complete conformity with the settled policy of the United States."

March 9: Secretary of State George Marshall instructs Warren Austin, United States representative to the United Nations, that if a United Nations special assembly on Palestine were convened, the United States would support a United Nations trusteeship for Palestine.

March 12: The United Nations Special Committee on Palestine reports that "present indications point to the inescapable conclusion that when the [British] mandate is terminated, Palestine is likely to suffer severely from administrative chaos and widespread strife and bloodshed."

March 13: President Truman's friend Eddie Jacobson walks into the White House without an appointment and pleads with Truman to meet with Chaim Weizmann, the president of the Jewish Agency for Palestine and the World Zionist Organization. Truman responds: "You win, you bald-headed son-of-a-bitch. I will see him."

March 18: President Truman meets with Chaim Weizmann, the president of the Jewish Agency for Palestine and the World Zionist Organization. Truman says he wishes to see justice done in Palestine without bloodshed, and that if the Jewish state were declared and the United Nations remained stalled in its attempt to establish a temporary trusteeship over Palestine, the United States would recognize the new state immediately.

March 19: United States Representative to the United Nations Warren Austin announces to the United Nations Security Council that the United States position is that the partition of Palestine is no longer a viable option.

March 20: President Truman, after learning of Ambassador Warren Austin's speech regarding the partition of Palestine at the United Nations the day before, writes this in his diary. "This morning I find that the State Dept. has reversed my Palestine policy. The first I know about it is what I see in the papers! Isn't that hell? I'm now in the position of a liar and a double-crosser: I never felt so in my life."

March 20: Secretary of State George Marshall announces that the United States will seek to work within the United Nations to bring a peaceful settlement to Palestine, and that the proposal for a temporary United Nations trusteeship for Palestine is the only idea presently being considered that will allow the United Nations to address the difficult situation in Palestine.

March 21: President Truman writes to his brother, Vivian Truman, regarding Palestine. "I think the proper thing to do, and the thing I have been doing, is to do what I think is right and let them all go to hell."

March 25: President Truman says at a press conference that a United Nations trusteeship for Palestine would be only a temporary measure, intended to establish the peaceful conditions that would be the essential foundation for a final political settlement. He says that trusteeship is not a substitute for partition.

April 11: President Truman's friend Eddie Jacobson enters the White House unnoticed via the east gate and meets with Truman. Jacobson recorded of this meeting. "He reaffirmed, very strongly, the promises he had made to Dr. Weizmann and to me; and he gave me permission to tell Dr. Weizmann so, which I did. It was at this meeting that I also discussed with the president the vital matter of recognizing the new state, and to this he agreed with a whole heart."

May 12: President Truman meets in the Oval Office with Secretary of State George Marshall, Undersecretary of State Robert Lovett, Counsel to the President Clark Clifford and several others to discuss the Palestine situation. Clifford argues in favor of recognizing the new Jewish state in accordance with the United Nations resolution of November 29, 1947. Marshall opposes Clifford's arguments and contends they are based on domestic political considerations. He says that if Truman follows Clifford's advice and recognizes the Jewish state, then he (Marshall) would vote against Truman in the election. Truman does not clearly state his views in the meeting.

May 12–14: Counsel to the President Clark Clifford and Undersecretary of State Robert Lovett discuss the different views held in the White House and the State Department regarding whether the United States should recognize the Jewish state. Lovett reports to Clifford on May 14 that Marshall will neither support nor oppose Truman's plan to recognize the Jewish state, that he will stay out of the entire matter.

May 13: Chaim Weizmann, president of the Jewish Agency for Palestine and the World Zionist Organization, writes to President Truman, "I deeply hope that the United States, which under your leadership has done so much to find a just solution [to the Palestine situation], will promptly recognize the Provisional Government of the new Jewish state. The world, I think, would regard it as especially appropriate that the greatest living democracy should be the first to welcome the newest into the family of nations."

May 14, late morning EST/late afternoon in Palestine: David Ben-Gurion, Israel's first prime minister, reads a "Declaration of Independence," which proclaims the existence of a Jewish state called Israel beginning on May 15, 1948, at 12:00 midnight Palestine time (May 14, 1948, 6:00 PM EST).

May 14, 6 PM EST/12:00 midnight in Palestine: The British mandate for Palestine expires and the State of Israel comes into being.

May 14, 6:11 PM EST/12:11 AM in Palestine: The United States recognizes Israel on a de facto basis. The White House issues the following statement: "This Government has been informed that a Jewish state has been proclaimed in Palestine, and recognition has been requested by the provisional government thereof. The

United States recognizes the provisional government as the de facto authority of the State of Israel."

May 14, shortly after 6:11 PM EST: United States Representative to the United Nations Warren Austin leaves his office at the United Nations and goes home. Secretary of State Marshall sends a State Department official to the United Nations to prevent the entire United States delegation from resigning.

May 15: Egypt, Syria, Jordan, Lebanon, and Iraq attack Israel.

1949

January 25: A permanent government takes office in Israel following popular elections.

January 31: The United States recognizes Israel on a de jure basis.

February 24–July 20, 1949: Israel signs armistice agreements with Egypt, Lebanon, Jordan, and Syria.

SELECTED BIBLIOGRAPHY

Acheson, Dean. *Present at the Creation: My Years in the State Department.* New York: Norton, 1969.

Ahmad, Ahar. "Islam and Democracy: Text, Tradition, History." *The American Journal of Islamic Social Science* 20, no. 1 (Winter 2003): 35–36.

Ali, Abdullah Yusuf. *The Holy Quran: Translation and Commentary.* Lahore, Pakistan: Islamic Propagation Center, 1934.

Barber, Benjamin. *Jihad vs. McWorld: How Globalism and Tribalism Are Reshaping the World.* New York: Ballantine Books, 1966.

Ben-Gurion, David. *Israel: A Personal History.* Translated by Nechemiah Meyers and Uzy Nystar. New York: Funk and Wagnall's, 1971.

de Bellaigue, Christopher, "Turkey's Hidden Past," *The New York Review of Books* 48, no. 4 (March 8, 2001): 38.

Benson, Michael T. *Harry S. Truman and the Founding of Israel.* Westport, CT: Praeger, 1997.

Bickerton, Ian. "President Truman's Recognition of Israel." *American Jewish Historical Quarterly* 58 (December 1968): 173–240.

Clifford, Clark, with Richard Holbrooke. *Counsel to the President: A Memoir.* New York: Random House, 1991.

Clifford, Clark. "Recognizing Israel: The behind-the-scenes struggle in 1948 between the President and the State Department." *American Heritage* 28, no. 3 (April 1977): 4–7, 10–11.

Cohen, Joshua. "Procedure and Substance in Deliberative Democracy." In *Democracy and Difference: Contesting the Boundaries of the Political,* edited by Seyla Benhabib, 95–119. Princeton, NJ: Princeton University Press, 1996.

Cohen, Michael J. *Palestine and the Great Powers, 1945–1948.* Princeton, NJ: Princeton University Press, 1982.

———. *Truman and Israel.* Berkeley: University of California Press, 1990.

Crum, Bartley C. *Behind the Silken Curtain.* New York: Simon and Schuster, 1947.

Daniels, Jonathan. *The Man of Independence.* Philadelphia: Lippincott, 1950.

Dinnerstein, Leonard. *America and the Survivors of the Holocaust.* New York: Columbia University Press, 1982.

Donovan, Robert J. *Conflict and Crisis: The Presidency of Harry S. Truman, 1945–1948.* New York: Norton, 1977.

Eban, Abba. *My Country: The Story of Modern Israel.* New York: Random House, 1972.

Engineer, Asghar Ali. *Religion and Liberation.* Jawahurnagar, Delhi: Ajanta Publishers, 1989.

Evensen, Bruce J. "The Limits of Presidential Leadership: Truman at War with Zionists, the Press, Public Opinion and His Own State Department over Palestine." *Presidential Studies Quarterly* 23 (Spring 1993): 269–87.

———. *Truman, Palestine, and the Press.* Westport, CT: Greenwood Press, 1992.

Fakhry, Majid. *An Interpretation of the Quran: English Translation and Meanings.* New York: New York University Press, 2004.

Feis, Herbert. *The Birth of Israel: The Tousled Diplomatic Bed.* New York: Norton, 1969.

Feiler, Bruce. *Abraham.* New York: Harper Collins, 2002.

Ferrell, Robert H. *Harry S. Truman: A Life.* Columbia: University of Missouri Press, 1994.

Ferrell, Robert H., ed. *Off The Record: The Private Papers of Harry S. Truman.* Columbia: University of Missouri Press, 1980.

Foreign Relations of the United States, The Near East and Africa, 1946 and 1947. Washington, DC: U.S. Government Printing Office, 1969, 1971.

Gann, Zvi. *Truman, American Jewry, and Israel, 1945–1948.* New York: Holmes and Meier, 1979.

Gardner, Michael. *Harry S. Truman and Civil Rights: Moral Courage and Political Risks.* Carbondale: Illinois University Press, 2002.

Green, Judith. *Deep Democracy: Community, Diversity and Transformation.* London: Rowan and Littlefield, 1999.

Hackman, Larry S., ed. *Harry S. Truman and the Recognition of Israel.* Independence, MO: Harry S. Truman Library, 1998.

Hamby, Alonzo L. *Beyond the New Deal: Harry S. Truman and American Liberalism.* New York: Columbia University Press, 1973.

———. *Man of the People: The Life of Harry S. Truman.* New York: Oxford University Press, 1995.

Hurewitz, J. C. *The Struggle for Palestine.* New York: Norton, 1950.

Kirkendall, Richard S., ed. *The Harry S. Truman Encyclopedia.* Boston: G. K. Hall, 1989.

Kramer, Joel. *Humanism in the Renaissance of Islam: The Cultural Revival during the Buyid Age.* Princeton, NJ: Darwin Press, 1985.

Lawson, Fred H. "Palestine." In Kirkendall, *Harry S. Truman Encyclopedia,* 269–70.

McCoy, Donald R. *The Presidency of Harry S. Truman.* Lawrence: University of Kansas Press, 1984.

McCullough, David. *Truman.* New York: Simon and Schuster, 1992.

Miller, Merle. *Plain Speaking: An Oral Biography of Harry S. Truman.* New York: Berkley Publishing, 1974.

Morris, Benny. *The Birth of the Palestinian Refugee Problem, 1947–1949.* Cambridge: Cambridge University Press, 1987.

Morse, Arthur,. *While Six Million Died: A Chronicle of American Apathy.* New York: Random House, 1968.

Neufeld, Michael J., and Michael Berenbaum, eds.*The Bombing of Auschwitz: Should the Allies have Attempted It.* New York: St Martin's Press, 2000.

Perry, Glenn. *The Middle East: 14 Islamic Centuries.* 3rd ed. Saddle River, NJ: Prentice Hall, 1997.

Pickthall, Mohammad Marmaduke. *The Meaning of the Glorious Quran.* New York: Mentor Book, n.d.

Podet, Allen Howard. *The Success and Failure of the Anglo-American Committee of Inquiry, 1945–1946.* Lewiston, NY: Edwin Mellen Press, 1986.

Postal, Bernard, and Henry W. Levy. *And the Hills Shouted for Joy: The Day Israel Was Born.* New York: McKay, 1973.

Rose, Norman. *Chaim Weizmann: A Biography.* New York: Viking, 1986.

Rosenthal, Franz. *The Classical Heritage in Islam.* London: Routledge, 1975.

Seger, Tom, with Arlen Neal Weinstein and Arlen N. Weinstein. *1949: The First Israelis.* New York: Henry Holt, 1986.

Snetsinger, John. *Truman, the Jewish Vote, and the Creation of Israel.* Stanford, CA: Hoover Institution Press, 1974.

Stevens, Richard P. *American Zionism and U.S. Foreign Policy, 1942–1947.* New York: Pageant, 1962.

Truman, Harry S. *Memoirs.* Vol. 1, *Year of Decisions.* New York: Doubleday, 1955.

Truman, Harry S. *Memoirs.* Vol. 2, *Years of Trial and Hope.* New York: Doubleday, 1956.

———. *Public Papers of the Presidents: Harry S. Truman, Containing the Public Messages, Speeches and Statements of the President. 1945–1953.* 8 vols. Washington, DC: U.S. Government Printing Office, 1961–66.

"Two Presidents and a Haberdasher." *American Jewish Archives* 20 (April 1968): 3–15.

Vanden Heuvel, William J. "America and the Holocaust." *American Heritage* 50, no. 4 (July–August 1999): 35–52.

Van Parijis, Phillipe, "Contestatory Democracy vs. Freedom for All." In *Democracy's Value,* edited by Ian Schapiro and Casiano Hacker Gordon, 191–98. Cambridge: Cambridge University Press, 1999.

Watzman, Hiam. *One Palestine, Complete: Jews and Arabs under British Mandate.* New York: Henry Holt, 2000.

Whom Shall We Welcome: Report of the President's Commission on Immigration and Naturalization. Washington, DC: Superintendent of Documents, January 1, 1953.

Wiesel, Elie. *Against Silence: The Voice and Vision of Elie Wiesel.* 3 vols. New York: Holocaust Library, 1985.

Wilson, Evan M. *Decision on Palestine: How the U.S. Came to Recognize Israel.* Stanford, CA: Hoover Institution Press, 1979.

CONTRIBUTORS

AHRAR AHMAD is professor of political science at Black Hills State University. He received his bachelor's degree from the University of Dhaka in Bangladesh and his PhD from Southern Illinois University. He has received grants for research and teaching from the National Endowment for the Humanities, the Chrisman Foundation, and the University Research Committee of South Dakota State University.

MICHAEL BENSON is the president of Snow College in Ephraim, Utah. He graduated from Brigham Young University with a BA in political science, and received his PhD from St. Anthony's College in Oxford in modern Middle Eastern history. He served as a development officer at the University of Utah (1995–98) and as special assistant to the president of the University of Utah (1998–2001). In addition to several journal articles, Benson is the author of *Harry S. Truman and the Founding of Israel.*

ALAN L. BERGER holds the Raddock Eminent Scholar Chair for Holocaust Studies and is a professor of Judaic studies at Florida Atlantic University. He graduated from University of Chicago Divinity School and received his PhD in humanities from Syracuse University. Prior to joining the faculty at Florida Atlantic University, he was a professor and chair of the department of religious studies at Syracuse University, where he founded and directed the Jewish studies program. He was the Gumenick Visiting Professor of Judaic Studies at the College of William and Mary (1988–89). The author of numerous works of scholarship on the Holocaust, he is coeditor of *Encyclopedia of Holocaust Literature* and author of *The Continuing Agony: From the Carmelite Convent to the Crosses at Auschwitz.*

WILLIAM A. BROWN served as United States ambassador to Israel under three presidents, Ronald Reagan, George H. W. Bush, and William Clinton. Following his graduation from Harvard (1952), he served in the United States Marine Corps, then returned to Harvard University where he earned his PhD (1963). He served as a State Department official in Hong Kong, Moscow, New Delhi, Taipei, and Tel Aviv. In Washington, DC, he has held positions as deputy director of the Office of Asian Communist Affairs and as special assistant to the administrator of the Environmental Protection Agency. From 1982 to 1985, he served as Principal Deputy Assistant to the Secretary of State for East Asian and Pacific Affairs.

MICHAEL J. DEVINE received his MA and PhD from Ohio State University. He is director of the Truman Presidential Museum and Library and president of the Harry S. Truman Library Institute. He has served as a senior Fulbright lecturer in Argentina (1983) and in Korea (1995), and was the Houghton Freeman professor at the Johns Hopkins Nanjing University Center in China (1998–99). In addition, Devine was the Illinois state historian (1985–91) and director of the American Heritage Center at the University of Wyoming (1991–2001).

ABBA EBAN (1915–2002), a statesman, author, and university lecturer, served as Israel's first ambassador to the United States from 1950 to 1959, and served simultaneously as Israel's permanent representative to the United Nations. First elected to the Israeli Knesset in 1959, he eventually served in that body for thirty years. From 1966 to 1974, he was minister of foreign affairs, and was a member of the Knesset's Committee on Foreign Affairs and Security from 1974 to 1988. Born in South Africa, he spent his early years in Great Britain and graduated from Cambridge University before serving in the British Army during World War II, attaining the rank of major.

GEORGE M. ELSEY served as a naval officer in the White House Map Room during World War II, and then as an aide to President Harry Truman. He played a key role in developing the Truman Doctrine, Truman's civil rights messages to Congress, and the executive orders that ended segregation in the armed forces. He is a graduate of Princeton University and earned a master's degree from Harvard University. Elsey has served as president of the American Red Cross and the White House Historical Association. He has also served as a trustee or director of the Brookings Institution, the National Geographic Society, and a number of other organizations. Among the many awards and honors he has received are the Order of the British Empire and the Order of St. John. He is the author of a memoir, *An Unplanned Life* (2005).

RAYMOND H. GESELBRACHT is special assistant to the director at the Harry S. Truman Library. He previously served as an archivist at the Franklin D. Roosevelt Library and the Richard M. Nixon Presidential Materials Project. He has published many articles on historical and archival subjects, including a recent series of articles on personal aspects of Truman's life and career. He has also published a descriptive map of places in the Kansas City area that were especially important to Truman, and a history of the Truman Library.

DAVID GORDIS is a rabbi and serves as president and professor of rabbinics at Hebrew College. He earned his BA and MA in history from Columbia University and his master's in Hebrew literature and PhD in Talmudic studies from the Jewish Theological Seminary of America. Prior to assuming the presidency of Hebrew College in 1993, he was vice president and provost at the University of Judaism in Los Angeles and lecturer in Jewish law at the University of California–Los Angeles. He has served as vice president of the Jewish Theological Seminary of America and vice president of the American Jewish Committee.

KEN HECHLER graduated from Swarthmore College with a BA, and received his MA and PhD from Columbia University. Prior to his military service in World War II, he served on the faculties of Columbia University, Princeton University, and Barnard College. He served in the White House of President Harry S. Truman from 1949 to 1953 as research director, speechwriter, and special assistant to the president. After his service in the Truman administration, Hechler was elected to nine terms in Congress (1959–77) as representative from West Virginia, and was elected to four four-year terms as West Virginia's secretary of state (1985–2001). He has written six books, including *The Bridge at Remagen,* which was made into a major motion picture.

JOHN JUDIS is a senior editor at the *New Republic*, where he has worked since 1984. He is currently serving as a visiting scholar at the Carnegie Endowment for International Peace in Washington, DC. Judis wrote *The Folly of Empire: What George W. Bush Could Learn from Theodore Roosevelt and Woodrow Wilson,* and his articles have appeared in *American Prospect, New York Times Magazine, The Washington Post, Foreign Affairs, Washington Monthly, American Enterprise, Mother Jones,* and *Dissent.* He has written five books, including *The Emerging Democratic Majority* (with Roy Teixeira), *The Paradox of American Democracy,* and *William F. Buckley: Patron Saint of the Conservatives.* Judis earned both his BA and MA from the University of California at Berkeley.

TOM LANSFORD is assistant dean of the College of Arts and Letters at the University of Southern Mississippi Gulf Coast. He received his BA from Virginia Wesleyan College, and his MA and PhD from Old Dominion University. He is a member of the governing board of the National Social Science Association, associate editor of the journal *White House Studies,* and book review editor for the *International Journal of Politics and Ethics.*

ASHER NAIM immigrated to Israel from Tripoli, Libya, and earned a master's of jurisprudence from Hebrew University. A veteran of Israel's War of Independence, he served as a diplomat in Tokyo (1956–60) and Kenya and Uganda (1961–64). In Washington, DC, he was an assistant to Ambassador Yitzhak Rabin as Councilor for Information and Culture (1968–73) and from 1976 to 1981 he served as Israeli consul general in Philadelphia. In 1984 he was assigned to Washington, DC, to coordinate the work of Israel's ten consuls general to the United States. He served as ambassador to Finland (1988–1990), Ethiopia (1990–91), and the United Nations (1991), and in 1992, he was appointed Israel's first ambassador to the Republic of Korea. Following his retirement from the Foreign Service in 1995, Ambassador Naim has served as the chairman of the Israel-Korea Friendship Association and as a fellow of the Truman Institute for Peace at Hebrew University in Jerusalem.

PAT SCHROEDER served twelve terms as a member of the U.S. House of Representatives from Colorado (1972-1996) and now serves as president and CEO of the Association of American Publishers. She graduated from the University of Minnesota with a BA degree in 1961 and earned a degree in law from Harvard University in 1964. Before entering a career in politics, she was a lawyer for the National Labor Relations Board and Planned Parenthood. A Democrat, she was the first woman member of the House Armed Services Committee. She also served on the House Judiciary Committee and the Post Office and Civil Service Committee. She chaired the House Select Committee on Children, Youth, and Families (1991–93) and cochaired the Congressional Caucus for Women's Issues.

ROBERT P. WATSON received his PhD from Florida Atlantic University. He is an associate professor of political science at Lynn University, and the author or editor of twenty-five books and over one hundred articles and chapters on the U.S. presidency, first ladies, campaigns, and elections. He is the founding editor of the journal *White House Studies.*

BRUCE WARSHAL is a rabbi with a degree in law from Yale University. He graduated with a degree in business from Wilkes College and earned a BA degree in Hebrew literature from Hebrew University. He teaches in the Lifelong Learning Society at Florida Atlantic University and has served on the Community Support Board for the Chair for Holocaust Studies at Florida Atlantic University.

ROBERT J. WOLZ is executive director of the Harry S. Truman Little White House in Key West, Florida. He is the author of *The Legacy of the Harry S. Truman Little White House: Presidents in Paradise,* and several articles on Florida history. Wolz is past vice commander-in-chief and national historian of the Sons of Union Veterans of the Civil War and a graduate of Youngstown State University. He is pursuing postgraduate studies in nonprofit management at Central Florida University.

INDEX